A GENTLE INTRODUCTION TO MUSIC APPRECIATION

BOB G. MAGEE, DMA

A gentle approach to music to create life-long music listeners

Fourth edition
May 2023

ACKNOWLEDGMENTS

I would like to express my sincere gratitude to the following during the publishing of *A Gentle Introduction to Music Appreciation.*

Dr. Robert G. Magee for encouragement, technical advice and formatting the text.

Mrs. Lynn Pennington for encouragement and content suggestions.

Dr. Chris Thompson for content suggestions and proofreading.

ISBN 9798386498092

Preface

Over 37 years' experience teaching music appreciation courses at the college level has shown me the need for a book that takes into consideration a student's interest and level of musical understanding and appreciation. My goal for this book is to provide a "gentle" introduction to music without the student's becoming overwhelmed. Many textbooks conduct students through a history of music which includes centuries of people, forms, genres, and developments without inspiring the student to delve further into how music might affect their daily lives. While music history is important, we do not experience music historically in our daily lives. Music comes to us by way of the Internet, radio, television, movie screen and other means. Music students are surprised to learn that classical music often is used commercially in radio and television.

My intent is not to present an exhaustive study of music history. Rather, my aim is twofold: (1) to offer a "gentle" approach to music that will create life-long music listeners who will understand and appreciate various types of music and who will realize how music affects their lives; (2) to provide a "crash" course in music that might help students prepare for an entrance exam required for a graduate music degree.

A Gentle Introduction to Music Appreciation is organized into six chapters: "Elemental Concepts of Music," "The Renaissance," "The Baroque," "The Classic Period," "Age of Romanticism," and "Music in the 20th Century and Later." Each chapter begins with a brief synopsis of the material to be presented. A study guide is included which can be used for individual review or to prepare for a test or exam. Musical terms are defined within the body of the text as well as in a detailed glossary located at the end. Non-English words are italicized. In each chapter, significant composers and personalities are presented along with selections of some of their most popular compositions. Internet listening suggestions are listed as ***Suggested Search***.

Table of Contents

Chapter I Elemental Concepts of Music

This chapter aids the student who is new to the study of music. The fundamentals of music, i.e., pitch, rhythm, melody, and harmony, are the basic materials composers use in creating their music compositions. The student will also become acquainted with the instruments of the orchestra and characteristic qualities of instruments and the human voice under the discussion timbre.

I. Sound

    A. Pitch - Highness or lowness of a musical sound.

        1. Tone A musical sound with a definite pitch.

        2. Staff - Five horizontal lines and four spaces on which music symbols are placed.

        3. Interval - Distance between two tones.

        4. Octave - An interval comprising the first and eighth notes of a major or minor scale; interval of an eighth, as from C to C.

    B. Dynamics, dynamic level - Loudness or softness of a tone.

        1. *Forte* - In musical notation, a dynamic marking meaning "loud." A connected term is called *Fortissimo* - In musical notation, a dynamic marking meaning "very loud."

        2. *Piano* - In musical notation, a dynamic marking meaning "soft." A connected term is called *Pianissimo* - In musical notation, a dynamic marking meaning "very soft." Piano is also the name of an instrument and is usually placed in the percussion section in an

3.   Orchestra. (See Keyboard Instruments)

4.   *Crescendo* - A gradual increase in the volume of sound.

5.   *Diminuendo, decrescendo* - A gradual decrease in the volume of sound.

6.   Terraced dynamics - A term used in the Baroque period to describe abrupt changes in dynamic levels.

Suggested Search:
    Music Theory: Dynamics Mr. Lefeber

    Also sprach Zarathustra, Richard Strauss

II.   Rhythm - Movement of music in time with recurring beats and accents.

    A. Beat - A recurring rhythmic pulse of music.

    B. Accent - Emphasis or stress placed on a musical beat.

    C. Meter - A term that denotes the organization of rhythm into patterns of strong and weak beats; often referred to as "time signature;" numbers such as 34 indicate the meter.

    D. Measure, bar - A rhythmic group of notes and rests located between bar lines on a staff.

    E. Tempo - The rate of speed at which a musical piece is performed, or relative pace of the music.

        1.   *Accelerando* - To gradually get faster; increase the pace.

2.   *Rallentando* - To gradually get slower; decrease the pace.

Suggested Search:
Pyotr Ilyich Tchaikovsky - Nutcracker Suite - Russian Dance Trepak - CMGR Orchestra

III.   Melody - A succession of notes perceived as a meaningful line.

     A. Diatonic scale (also known as a major scale) Name of a scale that consists of five whole steps and two half steps to form the familiar scale of Western music. The result is a seven-note pattern of tones that ascends in the following order of whole steps and half steps: 1 - 1 - ½ - 1 - 1 - 1 - ½. The major scale can be sung using the syllables: Do, Re, Mi, Fa, Sol, La, Ti, Do

     B. Minor scale - An ascending pattern of seven tones in the following order of whole steps and half steps: 1- ½ - 1 - 1- ½ - 1 - 1.

     C. Pentatonic scale - A five-note scale often found in folk music and non-western music.

     D. Chromatic scale - A scale that utilizes all twelve pitches, divided equally within the octave.

Suggested Search:
How To Read Piano Notes (Treble & Bass Clef) - Piano Lesson

     E. Sequence - A melodic phrase repeated at different pitch levels.

     F. Cadence - The close of musical phrase.

G. Tonic - The first and most important note of a major or minor scale, *Do*.

IV. Harmony - Simultaneous combination of notes which form chords.

    A. Chord - Three or more notes heard simultaneously as an entity that are meaningful.

    B. Triad - A chord consisting of at least three tones of intervals of a 3rd, i.e., C E G of a major scale.

    C. Dissonance - Two or more notes sounding together to produce "unsettled" sounds giving a feeling of unrest.

    D. Consonance - Interval or chord that has a pleasing, stable sound.

V. Musical Texture

Texture in a song refers to how the various parts or voices interact with each other to determine the nature, the quality of the song. There are three distinct types of texture that are most utilized in music: monophony, homophony, and polyphony.

    Suggested Search:
        Musical Textures *Row, Row, Row Your Boat* Youtube

    A. Monophony (monophonic music) - A single unaccompanied melodic line; can be sung by multiple voices.

    Suggested Search:
        What is a Monophonic Texture? Dave Conservatoire

        Music of the Middle Ages, Plainchant

    B. Homophony (homophonic music) - Musical texture in which a melody is accompanied by chords producing harmony.

Suggested Search:
> What is a HOMOPHONIC Texture? Dave Conservatoire
>
> HOMOPHONIC TEXTURE: Joyful, Joyful, We Adore Thee by Mormon Tabernacle Choir

C. Polyphony (polyphonic music) - A musical texture consisting of two or more melodies played simultaneously.

> Counterpoint - (See polyphony)

Suggested Search:
> What is a Polyphonic Texture? Dave Conservatoire
>
> When Jesus wep't the falling tear (1770), by William Billings (1746--1800)
>
> What is it? Is it Monophony, Homophony, or Polyphony?

VI. *Timbre* - The characteristic quality of an instrument or human voice.

A. Vocal timbres
1. Soprano - A high female singing voice.

2. Mezzo soprano - A medium-range female voice.

Suggested Search:
> Difference between vocal Soprano and mezzo-soprano

3. Alto, contralto - A low female voice or high male voice

Suggested Search:
>> Classical Female Voices Ajay CM

4.   Tenor - A high male voice.

Suggested Search:
>> Pavarotti- The Tenor Voice- If I were Only a Tenor!

5.   Baritone - A medium-range male voice.

6.   Bass - A low male voice

Suggested Search:
>> Classical Male Voices Ajay CM

7.   Unusual ranges

Suggested Search:
>> Ivan Rebroff Vocal Range (F1-A5)

>> Yma Sumac - Pachamama Carlos Arroyo
>>> (The above excerpt is from "Secret of the Incas" 1954.)

VII.   Terms

A. Band - A large instrumental ensemble consisting of brass, woodwind, and percussion instruments; this group is sometimes called a symphonic band.

B. Conductor - A person who leads performances of music ensembles such as bands, orchestras, or choirs.

C. Concertmaster - A member of the orchestra, usually the principal violinist, who is the assistant to the conductor.

D. *Opus* - Latin for "work." Opus numbers are used to indicate the chronological order in which a piece was composed.

E. Score - The notated parts for the instruments of an orchestra or voices in a musical composition.

F. Symphony - A large work for orchestra, usually consisting of four movements.

G. Symphony orchestra - A large instrumental ensemble consisting of the four families of instruments, strings, woodwinds, brass, and percussion; the string section is dominant.

VIII. Orchestral instruments

A. String Family - A family of instruments whose sound is produced by vibration of the strings either by plucking or bowing.

1. Violin - A string instrument with the highest range of the bowed string family.

2. Viola - A string instrument with a slightly lower range than the violin.

3. Cello - A bowed string instrument with a range lower than a viola and higher than a double bass. Originally called violoncello.

4. Double Bass - The largest member of the bowed string family, having the lowest range.

5. Harp - A plucked string instrument with the strings stretched over a frame in the shape of a triangle.

6.   Special effects for strings

    1. *pizzicato* - A technique where a performer plucks the strings of violin, viola, cello, or double bass rather than bowing.

    2. *col legno* - Where a performer plays a violin, viola, cello, or double bass with the wooden part of the bow.

    3. *tremolo* - String-playing technique by repeating the same pitch with quick up and down strokes on a violin, viola, cello, or double bass.

B. Woodwind Family - Instrumental family made of wood or metal whose sound is produced by vibrations of air in a tube; holes in the tube are opened and closed either by pads or fingers. Some woodwinds are played by blowing across a hole while others are played by blowing air into a mouthpiece which causes a reed or reeds to vibrate. Originally, these instruments were made only of wood.

    1.   Flute - A woodwind instrument, made of metal, with a high range; held horizontally, its tone is produced by blowing across a hole.

    2.   Piccolo - Smallest woodwind instrument having the highest range; like the flute but sounding one octave higher. It is a smaller version of the flute.

    3.   Oboe - A double-reed woodwind instrument with a medium-high range.

    4.   Clarinet - A single-reed woodwind instrument.

5.   Bassoon - A double-reed woodwind instrument with a low range and is the principal woodwind bass instrument in an orchestra.

6.   English horn - A double-reed woodwind instrument similar to the oboe. It is approximately one and a half times the length of an oboe and sounds lower in range.

7.   Saxophone - A single-reed instrument in the woodwind family usually used in jazz bands; not common in orchestras.

C. Brass Family - A family of instruments made of brass or silver whose sound is produced by buzzing the lips into a mouthpiece; the pitch is varied by valves or slides.

1.   Trumpet - The highest pitched brass instrument which changes pitch by depressing valves.

2.   Cornet - A brass instrument like the trumpet but with a more mellow tone.

3.   French horn - A brass instrument of a medium range whose tubing is coiled into a circle. It is played by depressing valves. Sometimes referred to as horn.

4.   Trombone - A brass instrument of a moderately low range with a movable slide to change pitch.

5.   Tuba - The largest brass instrument with the lowest range that changes pitch by depressing valves.

D. Percussion Family - A family of instruments of either definite or indefinite pitch whose sound is made by striking with hammer/stick, by shaking or by scraping.

1.	Timpani - A percussion instrument of definite pitch shaped like large copper upside-down kettles; played by mallets. A pedal mechanism changes the pitch. Sometimes called kettle drums.

2.	Chimes - A percussion instrument of definite pitch which consists of suspended metal tubes of various lengths that are struck with hammers.

3.	Cymbals - Percussion instruments of indefinite pitch consisting of two large plates that are struck together.

4.	Triangle - A percussion instrument of indefinite pitch consisting of a piece of metal bent in the shape of a triangle and is suspended from a cord; struck with a metal beater.

5.	Tambourine - A percussion instrument of indefinite pitch consisting of a round frame with pairs of small metal plates that jingle; played by shaking or striking.

6.	Xylophone - A percussion instrument of definite pitch consisting of flat blocks of wood laid on a frame; blocks are arranged in the shape of a keyboard and are played with wooden mallets.

7.	Snare drum - A percussion instrument of indefinite pitch. It is in the shape of a small cylinder with skin stretched over each end; a piece of metal mesh is attached to the lower skin which causes a rattling sound when struck.

8.   Bass drum - A percussion instrument of indefinite pitch played with a large soft mallet; the largest drum in band or orchestra.

Suggested Search:
Young Person's Guide - Britten Symphony Orchestra 2011

IX.   Keyboard Instruments
   A. Piano - An acoustic, stringed musical instrument invented in Italy by Bartolomeo Cristofori around the year 1700, in which the strings are struck by hammers; pedals control dampers on the strings that stop the sound when the keys are released. Listed in the percussion family because of its location within the orchestra.

   B. *Pianoforte* or *fortepiano* - A keyboard instrument invented in early 1700's that uses a mechanism to strike the strings and so named because of the ability to vary the tone from "soft to loud" by using pedals and dampers; this is one of the main differences from the harpsichord. This instrument is commonly referred to today as a piano.

   C. Harpsichord - A popular keyboard instrument of the Baroque and Classic periods; its strings were plucked by a small plectrum or quill; sometimes called *cembalo*.

        Suggested Search:
                Elaine Comparone, Introduction to the Harpsichord

D. Pipe organ - A large instrument comprised of several keyboards (manuals) and ranks of tuned pipes of assorted sizes. When a key is depressed, air is forced through the pipes which generates pitches. Many consider the pipe organ to be "king of all instruments."

Suggested Search:
> How an Organ Makes Music Duke Chapel
>
> The Wanamaker Organ - Inside the world's largest operating musical instrument

Chapter II The Renaissance, 1450-1600

Chapter II, "The Renaissance, 1450-1600," will give the student a better understanding of the movements Humanism and the Protestant Reformation. Both sacred music and secular music of the Renaissance will be treated. Reformists Martin Luther and John Calvin will be presented along with their influence on sacred music in the Lutheran and Calvinist churches. The effects of the Renaissance on the music of the Catholic Church and the influence of Palestrina will be discussed. This chapter will acquaint the student with polyphony and related terminology used in the mass, motet, and madrigal.

Renaissance, which means "rebirth" in French, was not a musical style, but rather describes the activity and time of the revival of art and literature in Europe beginning in the 14th century and extending to the 17th century. Many scholars consider this period as marking the transition from the medieval to the modern world. The Renaissance was significantly affected by two movements: Humanism and the Protestant Reformation. Humanism emphasized the value and goodness of human beings and recognized an individual's dignity and worth as well as the ability to think and reason for oneself.

The Protestant Reformation, a religious movement begun by Martin Luther of the 16th century (1517), was an attempt to reform the Roman Catholic Church; this resulted in the founding of Protestant churches. The Protestant Reformation brought new types of religious music including the chorale and the psalter. Connected with the Protestant reformation was the counter-reformation, which began with the Council of Trent to address issues within the Roman Catholic Church. Also, the newly developed movable type printing process introduced the era of mass communication, which significantly impacted society by allowing for a wider distribution of written materials for an increasing market.

Suggested Search:
Renaissance Music Overview Caroline Simyon

I. Three significant influences on the Renaissance:

   a. Humanism
       A movement during the Renaissance that stressed the potential value and goodness of human beings along with a renewed interest in ancient art and cultures. This movement originated in northern Italy during the 13th and 14th centuries and later spread through continental Europe and England. Emphasis was placed on the value of human beings, individually and collectively and focused on critical thinking and evidence over acceptance of tradition or superstition.

   b. Protestant Reformation
       A religious movement inadvertently begun by Martin Luther in the 16th century that was an attempt to reform the Roman Catholic Church; resulted in the founding of Protestant churches. The Protestant Reformation brought new types of religious music including the chorale and psalters.

      i. Counter Reformation
          The period the Roman Catholic Church initiated in response to the Protestant Reformation; it began with the Council of Trent.

      ii. Council of Trent
           Prompted by the Protestant Reformation, the Council of Trent was primarily responsible for self-reform in the Roman Catholic Church. It played a vital role in revitalizing the Roman Catholic Church in many parts of Europe.

c. Printing Press

The printing press, invented by Johann Gutenberg during the Renaissance, forever changed the lives of people in Europe and, eventually, all over the world. Previously, producing books involved copying all the words and illustrations by hand. The labor that went into creating them made each book expensive. Because Gutenberg's press could produce books with less labor involved and rapidly, publishing books became much less expensive; more people were able to buy reading material.

II. Sacred Music of the Renaissance

Sacred Music of the Renaissance was centered in the Roman Catholic Church and is sometimes referred to as "The Golden Age of Polyphony." Much of the sacred music of the Renaissance was both Polytextual (the simultaneous use of more than one text in a single vocal composition) and Polylingual (multilingual; using several languages in the same composition). For example: a motet consisting of three voices sung in the Roman Catholic Church might contain the texts: "Praise to the Virgin Mary" sung by the top voice in Latin; "Forgive us our sins" sung by the middle voice in Latin; and "Praise to the Holy Trinity" sung by the bottom voice in French.

a. Types of Roman Catholic Church music

i. Mass - The primary worship service of the Roman Catholic Church; a musical setting of the Ordinary of the Mass, i.e., *Kyrie, Gloria, Credo, Sanctus*, and *Agnus Dei*.

ii. Motet - Polyphonic vocal form. The exact meaning of motet changes during music history. After the 15th century, any polyphonic setting of a sacred text in Latin (not Mass) could be called a motet.

III.   Reformists during the Renaissance

    a. Martin Luther

Martin Luther was a German professor of theology, composer, priest, and a significant figure in the Protestant Reformation. The Protestant Reformation began when he posted a document which he called "The Disputation on the Power of Indulgences," which became known as "Luther's 95 Theses." This was a list of 95 grievances he had against the Roman Catholic Church. His intent was to invite the Church Fathers to debate these issues with him. Among those grievances was the use of polyphony in worship. He considered polyphony too complex (polytextual, polylingual), too ornate, and two difficult to be used effectively in worship.

As a composer, Luther introduced the chorale to Lutheran congregations during the Protestant Reformation. He introduced the chorale to congregational worship so people could readily participate in singing. The chorale text was set to a familiar melody, or one that was easily learned by the congregation. The chorale consisted of several stanzas in strophic form, like hymns used in many Protestant churches. *Ein feste Burg ist unser Gott* ("A Mighty Fortress is our God") is Luther's most famous chorale.

    i. Chorale - A type of hymn sung by the congregation in the Lutheran Church; introduced by Martin Luther.

      1. Stanza - A group of lines forming the basic recurring metrical unit in a poem; sometimes referred to as verse.

      2. Through-composed - A song form that has new music for each stanza.

3. Strophic - A song form that has two or more stanzas to the same music.

ii. *Ein feste Burg ist unser Gott* ("A Mighty Fortress is our God")

Suggested Search:
Thomanerchor Leipzig | "Ein feste Burg ist unser Gott" (EG Lied 362) | Trauerfeier Kurt Masur (2016)

"A Mighty Fortress Is Our God" - Mormon Youth Chorus

HeartSong Cedarville University - A Mighty Fortress (Official Music Video)

ANECDOTE:
When Martin Luther worked in his study, he often refused food and preferred to stay locked inside. On one occasion, a friend arrived with some musicians to visit him. When he did not answer the door, they broke open the door and found Luther lying on the floor unconscious. They lifted Luther up, began to sing and slowly he regained consciousness. Before long, he began to sing with them. He implored his friends to visit him often; he believed that a Satanic presence and sadness left him as soon as he heard music.

b. John Calvin
John Calvin was an influential French theologian, pastor, and reformer during the Protestant Reformation. He proposed reforms in church music that required only a cappella singing of the Psalms.

Calvin set all 150 psalms to music for the congregation to sing. The **psalter**, a collection of psalms set to meter and rhyme, was all that was allowed to be used in worship.

IV. Sacred Music After the Counter Reformation

Characteristics of Roman Catholic Church Music
  i. Sacred – Connected with God or dedicated to a religious purpose.

  ii. Sung in Latin

  iii. Polyphonic

  iv. Male voices

  v. A cappella – "In Chapel Style." Singing without instrumental accompaniment

Palestrina
Giovanni Pierluigi, born in Palestrina, Italy, took the name of his hometown as his surname and became known as "Palestrina." He was choir boy, and later, organist/choirmaster at several churches in Palestrina. He composed more masses for the Roman Catholic Church than any other composer and is recognized as the outstanding composer of the late Renaissance.

Many of the concerns Martin Luther mentioned in his "95 Theses" were related to polyphonic music. The Council of Trent intended to banish all polyphony from Roman Catholic Church liturgy. Palestrina composed a six-voice polyphonic mass entitled *Missa Papae Marcelli* (Mass for Pope Marcellus) in which he demonstrated that the texts of polyphonic music could be understood. He is often referred to as "the Savior of Church Music."

Suggested Search:
> Mass for Pope Marcellus: Agnus Dei I by
> Giovanni Palestrina

V. Secular music of the Renaissance
During the Renaissance, secular vocal music became popular and was readily available to most families due to the development of the printing press. As music was such an important part of leisure time, every educated person was expected to know how to sing and play an instrument.

    a. Madrigal
One of the most prominent secular forms of music during the Renaissance was the madrigal, a polyphonic and/or homophonic secular song begun in Italy during the 14th century, which also became popular in England. The madrigal was written either for solo voice or for groups of several voices and used a technique called text painting or word painting, a technique that uses music to describe images in the text, such as a minor key to portray sadness or an ascending scale when the text speaks of rising or climbing.

Suggested Search:
> Madrigal: *As Vesta was from Latmos Hill-*
> Thomas Weelkes

    b. Lute
Instruments during the early Renaissance typically accompanied singing or dancing. Eventually, instruments became from accompanying to that of performing solo. Renaissance composers began to create solo music for the lute, a plucked string instrument most widely used during the Middle Ages, Renaissance, and Baroque periods.

The lute characteristically had a pear-shaped body with a rounded back. John Dowland was an English Renaissance composer, accomplished lutenist, and singer. He is well known today for his melancholy songs but his compositions for **lute** are a current source of repertoire for lutenists and classical guitarists.

Suggested Search:
Ophira Zakai - Renaissance Lute

c. Harpsichord
    The harpsichord was a popular keyboard instrument of the Baroque and Classic periods; its strings were plucked by a small plectrum or quill; sometimes called cembalo. (See Harpsichord in Chapter I)

d. Clavichord
    Another popular instrument during the Renaissance was the clavichord, a small keyboard instrument that produces a soft sound and used mostly in private homes. The tone is created by a small metal blade that strikes the strings. The clavichord is smaller than the harpsichord.

    Suggested Search:
    Prelude for Clavichord in C major (2011) by Eduardo Antonello -New Baroque Music

VI. Dances of Renaissance
    During the Renaissance period, much of the entertainment consisted of dances. Country dances and court dances were different. Court dances were choreographed and were for entertainment by the upper class and often required training; country dances were more spontaneous and enjoyed by anyone. A Renaissance dance can be compared to a ball. The dances ranged from slow, stately dances (*barriera, pavane, allemande*) to fast, lively dances (*galliard, courante*).

Suggested Search:

How to Dance Through Time: The Majesty of Renaissance Dance | Dancetime

Pavane - Galliard

Barriera (Renaissance Dance)

Chapter III The Baroque, 1600-1750

In Chapter III, "The Baroque, 1600-1750," the student will gain a broad knowledge of the characteristics of Baroque music. An important attribute of this time was the interest in drama, which led to the development of opera, oratorio, and cantata. In addition, new instrumental systems and forms were developed. Among those are: figured bass, suite, fugue, concerto grosso, and concerto. Major composers that will be discussed include Claudio Monteverdi, Henry Purcell, G.F. Handel, J.S. Bach, and Antonio Vivaldi.

Baroque is a term given to a style of European architecture, music, and art of the 17th and 18th centuries characterized by ornate detail. The term Baroque comes from the Portuguese word "barroco" meaning "imperfect pearl." Baroque was applied to anything considered exaggerated, odd, irregular, complex or rough. It was not a complimentary term. It was used to describe music and other artistic expressions with complex forms, excessive ornamentation and anything exaggerated. In architecture the period is demonstrated by the palace of Versailles and by the work of Lorenzo Bernini, architect and sculptor in Italy.

Suggested Search:
Baroque Music Overview Caroline Simyon

Music in the Baroque Period was both sacred and secular and followed two styles (solo or monody, and choral or polyphony). The Florentine Camerata was a group of intellectuals in Florence, Italy who met regularly during mid-1500's and believed that polyphony was inadequate to express drama effectively. They argued that only a single melodic line, sung by a solo voice, could effectively portray poetry and drama.

This led to a new genre of music called monody, solo song accompanied by one or more instruments (not to be confused with monophony, a single unaccompanied melodic line sung by multiple voices).

This interest in drama eventually led to the development of opera, and later, oratorio and cantata.

1. Monody - A solo song accompanied by one or more instruments.

2. Libretto - Text of an opera, oratorio, cantata, or other dramatic work.

3. Recitative - A type of vocal singing that approximates natural speech inflections accompanied by a keyboard, usually harpsichord; used in opera, oratorio, and cantata. The words are sung quickly, often on repeated notes.

4. Aria - Vocal solo in an opera, oratorio, or cantata with orchestral accompaniment. In an operatic aria, the words, "I seek revenge" might be sung several times to fully express the emotion of the moment. Unlike the Recitative, the aria, with a melody, could last for several minutes.

> *Suggested Search:*
>> *Rodelinda* G.F. Handel– Act 2 recitative and aria
>>
>> "Then Shall The Eyes Of The Blind Be Opened/He Shall Feed His Flock" - Handel's *Messiah.*

I. Claudio Monteverdi
    Claudio Monteverdi was an Italian composer, singer, and Catholic priest. He is recognized as a transitional composer living between the Renaissance and the Baroque periods of music history.

    While Monteverdi worked in the tradition of earlier Renaissance polyphony, he also was the first composer of operatic masterpieces during the Baroque.

In Monteverdi/s dramatic music, he used the basso continuo technique, distinctive of the Baroque. Monteverdi composed one of the earliest operas still regularly performed, *L'Orfeo*, 1607.

Brief synopsis of *L'Orfeo*: Orpheus and Eurydice are married, but later Eurydice is bitten by a snake and dies. Orpheus travels to the Underworld determined to bring her back to life. He convinces Hades to let Eurydice go but her release comes with a condition. She must walk behind as they ascend, and Orpheus is forbidden to look at her. As they reach the exit, Orpheus turns to look at Eurydice and she is immediately cast back into the Underworld. Orpheus spends the rest of his life mourning her and singing sad songs.

Suggested Search:
"Tu Se Morta" - *L'Orfeo* - Monteverdi

While Renaissance polyphony was prevalent in the early Baroque, another type of choral music evolved: Polychoral (sometimes referred to as antiphonal). Polychoral is the name of the style; antiphonal is the effect.

1. Polychoral - Vocal or instrumental music for two or more choirs that perform alternately; characteristic of the music performed in St. Mark's Cathedral, Venice, Italy.

2. Antiphonal - A term which describes a performance in which two or more groups alternate singing or playing instruments.

3. Terraced dynamics - A term used in the Baroque period to describe abrupt changes in dynamic levels; first associated with St. Mark's Cathedral.

St. Mark's Cathedral (Basilica) was under construction for over 500 years. This resulted in many balconies and alcoves throughout the edifice. Choirs of instruments were placed on these balconies to create an antiphonal effect. This arrangement of performing choirs of instruments became known as polychoral music.

> *Suggested Search:*
> Inside St Mark's Basilica - Venice, Italy

II. Giovanni Gabrieli
Giovanni Gabrieli, an Italian composer, and organist, was one of the most dominant musicians of his time. He wrote many compositions for St. Mark's Cathedral in polychoral style. One of his most famous compositions is *Sonata pian e forte* for brass.

> *Suggested Search:*
> Giovanni Gabrieli - *Sonata pian e forte* - Compass Rose Brass Ensemble

III. Henry Purcell
Henry Purcell, an English composer, is one of the greatest English composers of the Baroque era. Purcell wrote a large amount of music for keyboard and chorus, and operas. The opera, *Dido and Aeneas* is recognized as one of his greatest works. In *Dido and Aeneas,* Purcell utilized a musical idea often found in Baroque works in which the bass is repeated over and over while the melody above it changes. This is called a ground bass.

Brief synopsis of *Dido and Aeneas*: The libretto of *Dido and Aeneas* was inspired by Aeneid, a poem written by the Roman poet, Virgil around 70 B.C. In his account, Aeneas was shipwrecked on the shore of Carthage where Dido was queen.

While Aeneas and his men were in Carthage, Dido fell in love with Aeneas, and they became husband and wife. When the gods command Aeneas to leave Carthage, Dido is heartbroken and decides her own fate.

Suggested Search:
    Purcell- *Dido and Aeneas*; "Thy Hand Belinda", "When I am Laid", "With Drooping Wings"

Renaissance composers did not specify which instruments were to play which part. In any given piece, each part could be played on any instrument which had a similar range. Individual instrumental sonorities were of no primary concern if the part could be played. This new concept led to idiomatic writing, music that is written for a specific instrument, considering the instrument's special capabilities, i.e., range, timbre.

IV.   Antonio Vivaldi
    Antonio Vivaldi is recognized as the best-known composer of concertos during the Baroque period, having composed over 450. In addition to composing, he was violinist, teacher, and Catholic priest. As priest, he was responsible for teaching music to orphaned children in Venice. He composed concertos for the violin, viola, and a variety of other instruments. His best-known work is a series of four violin concertos known as *The Four Seasons*. Each concerto depicts a season of the year and is accompanied by a poem written by Vivaldi. Of *The Four Seasons*, the concerto "Spring" is the most popular. Each of these concertos depicts sounds typically associated with one of the seasons of the year. These concertos, "Spring," "Summer," "Autumn," and "Winter" are considered forerunners of program music that became popular during the Romantic period (See Chapter V).

   1. Concerto grosso - A multi-movement instrumental work that uses a small ensemble of solo instruments along with a larger group of instruments. Some

scholars say *The Four Seasons* mark a transition from the concerto grosso to the more modern concerto.

Suggested Search:
>
> Vivaldi *Concerto Grosso in D minor*, Op. 3 No. 11

2. Concerto - A multi-movement work for orchestra and an instrumental soloist.
   The Four Seasons

   In the *Four Seasons* "Spring," listen for birds, summer breezes, thunderstorms, and lightning. Some scholars consider this to be a forerunner of Program Music.

   Suggested Search:
   >
   > Vivaldi, *The Four Seasons*, "Spring" (La Primavera), 1st movement
   >
   > Michala Petri and Kremerata Baltica plays Vivaldi: Recorder concerto 443 3.Movement

V. Opera

The first public opera house opened in Venice, Italy in 1637. Now anyone, regardless of social class, could attend an opera performance. During one season, there were six full-time opera houses in operation. Operas (opera seria, "serious opera") throughout Italy became enormous attractions utilizing special effects such as gods descending on clouds, ships tossed by stormy seas, erupting volcanoes, all manipulated by special machinery.

The Baroque marked the beginning of the virtuoso singer, namely the castrato. In addition to becoming a great attraction to the public, opera significantly affected the Italian economy due to the extra musicians, carpenters, tailors, printers, and food brokers required by opera performances.

1. Castrato - Male singer castrated before puberty to preserve the high vocal range, prominent during the 17th and 18th centuries, especially in opera and oratorio. Farinelli was an Italian castrato singer of the 18th century and one of the greatest singers in the history of opera.

    Bel canto - "Beautiful singing." Elegant Italian vocal style of the early 19th century that emphasized the beauty and virtuosity of the human voice; typically associated with the castrato.

2. Oratorio - Genre of dramatic vocal music based on a religious theme, usually taken from the Old Testament, that originated in the 17th century; performed in concert style, it was like an opera with no acting, costumes nor scenery.

3. Oratory - Prayer chapel; oratorios were first performed in prayer chapels rather than in concert halls or private homes. Hence, the name oratorio.

4. Ballad opera - Genre of 18th-century comic plays popular in England and Ireland featuring songs in English. The texts were usually satirical poking fun at English political or social life and Italian opera, immensely popular in London at that time.

    Ballad Opera began as an intermezzo inserted between the acts of opera seria. To keep the audience from becoming restless during the changing of scenery and costumes, small groups sang songs, and performed skits.

VI.   George Frideric Handel

G.F. Handel (1685-1759) was truly an international musician and composer. He was born in Germany, lived in Italy for a time, and eventually became a British citizen. Handel's greatest success as an opera composer occurred while he lived in England. Handel opened three commercial opera companies to produce opera seria, (Italian opera) for the English nobility.

One of Handel's earliest operas he composed while in London was *Xerxes*. The opera opens with the King of Persia singing a song to a tree, thanking it for its shade: "Ombra mai fu." In Handel's production, this role was sung by a castrato but is sung by a female or a countertenor today.

Suggested Search:
    "Ombra Mai Fu" *Xerxes* Cécilia Bartoli

Italian opera in London was entertainment enjoyed primarily by the London aristocracy. The middle-class public had no desire to attend performances of mythological stories sung in a foreign language. The middle-class audience preferred a new type of entertainment called ballad opera. Eventually, the popularity of opera seria declined and Handel turned his attention to another genre: oratorio.

Even though Handel composed approximately 40 operas, he is internationally recognized today for the oratorio, *Messiah*, regarded by many to be the world's best-loved and best-known oratorio. According to his own diary, he completed the rough draft of *Messiah* in approximately 24 days, working as if possessed. *Messiah* depicts the of life of Christ from the Old and New Testaments and is divided into three sections: (1) Prophecy (2) Fulfillment and (3) Thanksgiving.

The first performance of *Messiah* took place in Dublin, Ireland in 1741; the occasion was a benefit to raise money to free men from debtors' prison. During the first London performance of *Messiah* in 1743, King George II stood up as soon as the choir sang the "Hallelujah" chorus at the words "For the Lord God omnipotent reigneth" and remained standing during the rest of the chorus. Audiences continue to stand when this famous chorus is performed.

Suggested Search:
   Handel: Messiah, Hallelujah (Sir Colin Davis, Tenebrae, LSO)

ANECDOTE:
   Once when Handel was accompanying an English singer on the harpsichord, the singer complained about Handel's accompanying abilities. The singer threatened that if Handel did not improve his accompanying techniques, he would jump up and down on the harpsichord. Handel replied: "Please let me know when you will do that, and I will advertise. I'm sure the people had rather watch you jump than hear you sing."

VII.   Johann Sebastian Bach
   J.S. Bach (1685-1750), born in Germany, is regarded by many musicologists as the greatest composer of all time. He was known during his lifetime primarily as an outstanding organ player, technician, church musician and teacher.

   Bach was not recognized as a great composer during his lifetime. By the time of his death, Baroque tastes in music began to wane; people preferred light uncomplicated music. With his death in 1750, musicologists mark the end of the **Baroque** age in music.

   A devout Lutheran, Bach composed a great many **sacred** works as his duties required when he was employed by the St. Thomas Church in Leipzig.

Bach customarily wrote initials at the beginnings and endings of many of his compositions: JJ - *Jesu juva* (Jesus Help), SDG - *Soli Deo Gloria* (To God Alone be Glory), and INJ - *In Nomine Jesu* (In the Name of Jesus).

1. Types of J. S. Bach's vocal and choral works

   i. Cantata - In the 17th and 18th centuries, a vocal chamber work on a religious or secular subject that included several movements with recitatives and arias; shorter than an oratorio.

      Bach was familiar with cantatas and how they formed an integral part of the Lutheran Church worship service. According to the liturgical year, many Sundays required their own cantata. A typical Lutheran church service would consist of chorales, scripture readings, a short motet, a sermon, and a cantata. That, in addition to special occasions and holidays, resulted in approximately 60 cantatas per year. About 200 of his known sacred cantatas survive in addition to numerous secular cantatas.

      Suggested Search:
      Best Version of "Jesu, Joy Of Man's Desiring" by Bach (With Lyrics)

      J.S. Bach - Chorus "Gloria in excelsis Deo" from Cantata BWV 191

      Johann Sebastian Bach - "Coffee Cantata" BWV 211 (English Subtitles)

   ii. Passion - A musical setting of the arrest, trial, and crucifixion of Jesus based on the accounts taken from the New Testament; similar to oratorio and cantata in style.

Bach composed five passions, one based on each of the four gospels Matthew, Mark, Luke, and John in the New Testament; the fifth was based upon a compilation of texts. Only two passions remain, *St. John Passion* and *St. Matthew Passion.*

Suggested Search:
Bach Matthew "Passion Chorale" Settings - O Haupt voll Blut und Wunden

iii. Motet - polyphonic vocal form. The exact meaning of motet changes during music history. After the 15th century, any polyphonic setting of a sacred text in Latin (not mass) was called a motet.

1. Bach composed at least six motets, some for double chorus. While some of his motets were used in the Lutheran worship service, it is believed that others were for funerals. One of his most popular motets is *Komm, Jesu, Komm* ("Come, Jesus, Come") for double chorus.

Suggested Search:
Bach - *Motet Komm, Jesu, komm...* BWV 229 - MacLeod | Netherlands Bach Society

2. J. S. Bach's music for keyboards (Clavier).

i. Clavier - A generic term for any musical instrument having a keyboard such as a harpsichord, clavichord, or piano.

ii. Prelude - An introductory piece for a keyboard, usually short.

iii. Fugue - A polyphonic composition based on a theme (subject) with successive statements of the theme at different pitches.

iv. Basso continuo - A form of musical accompaniment used in the Baroque period made up of a bass part, usually played by cello, throughout a piece while a keyboard (usually harpsichord or other chord-playing instrument) played the harmony. It means "continuous bass."

v. Figured bass – Writing and copying music required a great deal of time in the Baroque period so a system of musical "shorthand" was developed in which a melody and an instrumental bass line are written on a staff. Another instrument, such as harpsichord or lute, then fills in the harmony by playing the figured bass, i.e., numbers, sharps or flats written beneath the staff to indicate the chords to be played.

vi. Equal temperament - A system of tuning in which the octave is divided into 12 equal half-steps (semitones); the most common system of tuning for Western music.

> *Suggested Search:*
> Well Tempered Tuning explained by Bach

1. *The Well-Tempered Clavier* by J.S. Bach is a collection of preludes and fugues demonstrating a new tuning system for keyboard instruments (tempered - earlier term for tuned).

Issued in two collections, *The Well-Tempered Clavier* consists of a prelude and fugue in each of the twelve major and twelve minor keys, making a total of 48 preludes and fugues.

Suggested Search:
Brink Bush performs "Little Fugue in G minor" BWV 578 - J.S. Bach

3. J. S. Bach's orchestral music

The Brandenburg Concertos are a collection of six instrumental works presented by Bach to Christian Ludwig, Military Governor of Brandenburg, Germany. They are regarded as some of the best orchestral works of the Baroque period.

Suggested Search:
Bach - Brandenburg Concerto No. 2 in F major BWV 1047 - 3. Allegro assai

ANECDOTE:
When J.S. Bach worked as a teacher in Arnstadt, he got into trouble with the authorities over a public disturbance with a student. The student had accused Bach of ridiculing him in public during a rehearsal and called Bach 'a dirty dog.' He struck Bach in the face; Bach drew his sword and only the intervention of another student prevented a public dual. When Bach complained to the authorities, he was reprimanded and reminded that he was at fault for having called the student 'a nanny-goat bassoonist' during the rehearsal.

VIII. Chamber Music
During the Baroque, chamber music, music for a small group performed in a home or small auditorium and with one player to a part, was played primarily by amateur musicians in their homes. Eventually, chamber music moved from the

home to the concert hall. A popular instrument combination for chamber music consisted of violin (I and II), viola, and cello. The violin became the most popular instrument of the Baroque period.

1. Violin Makers of the Baroque Period

   i. Nicolo Amati (1596-1684)
     Nicolo Amati was the first well-known *luthier* (maker of string instruments) of the Baroque period. He was the teacher of Giuseppi Guarneri del Gesu and Antonio Stradivari.

   ii. Giuseppi Guarneri del Gesu (1638-1744)
     Giuseppi Guarneri del Gesu, often referred to as "Del Gesus," was born into a celebrated family of violin makers in Cremona, Italy. He is recognized today as one of the greatest violin makers of the Baroque period. Many professional violinists consider them to be equal in quality to those of Antonio Stradivari. Two hundred Del Gesus violins survive.

Suggested Search:
     Paganini's Violin-1706 Guarneri

   iii. Antonio Stradivari (1644-1737)
     Antonio Stradivari, Cremona, Italy, was a craftsman of string instruments such as violins, violas, cellos, guitars, and harps. He is considered one of the most significant and greatest makers of string instruments during the Baroque period. His instruments are known by the name Stradivarius, which is the Latinized form of his surname, Stradivari. He produced over 1,000 instruments, mostly violins; 650 violins survive.

Suggested Search:
> That's Why Stradivarius Violins Are
> So Expensive

> Hear a $15 Million Stradivarius | Now
> Hear This | Great Performances on
> PBS

The value of the violins depends upon the taste and preference of the performer and/or the collector. Some authorities say the Stradivari violins have a higher frequency, closer to tenors while the Guarneri and Amati both have frequencies similar to baritone singers.

Relax and enjoy two Minutes of Stradivari Amati & Guarneri.

Suggested Search:
> 2 Minutes of Stradivari Amati & Guarneri

Chapter IV The Classic Period, 1750-1825

Chapter IV, "The Classic Period, 1750-1825," begins with a brief description of the Rococo sub period, which overlapped the late Baroque and early Classic periods. In the treatment of the Classic period, attention is given to the structure of instrumental music. Various forms are listed along with connected terms. Comic opera and a brief discussion of sacred music is presented. The lives and careers of Wolfgang Amadeus Mozart and Franz Josef Haydn are discussed.

> *Suggested Search:*
> Classic Music Overview Caroline Simyon

The dates of the Classic period are generally accepted as being between the year 1750 and the year 1825. Classic music is less complex than Baroque music and has a lighter, clearer texture. Instrumental music received substantial attention by Classic period composers. The principal kinds of instrumental music were the sonata, string quartet, symphony, and the solo concerto. The pianoforte eventually replaced the harpsichord as the main keyboard instrument. The significant form or structure for nearly all instrumental music of this period was the sonata-allegro form; this term was eventually shortened to sonata form (this should not be confused with sonata, a multi-movement piece to be played on an instrument).

Vocal music (choral works and opera), while dominated by instrumental music, was also important during this period. The Classic period saw the development of comic opera. The best-known composers from this period are Franz Joseph Haydn, Wolfgang Amadeus Mozart, Ludwig van Beethoven, and Franz Schubert. Ludwig van Beethoven and Franz Schubert are considered transitional figures since they composed during both the Classic and Romantic periods. They will be discussed in the next chapter.

I.   Rococo (French)

Rococo is a French 18th-century artistic movement, which affected many aspects of the arts. Painting, sculpture, architecture, literature, music, and theater were all impacted by the Rococo. It developed as a reaction to the strict regulations of the Baroque style. Rococo artists and architects used a florid, graceful approach to the Baroque. Their ornate style used light colors and curves with frivolous and witty themes. The interior decoration of Rococo rooms featured elegant, ornate furniture, small sculptures, ornamental mirrors, and wall paintings.

The Rococo love of shell-like curves and focus on decorative arts gave the impression that the style was superficial and not serious. It originated in Paris but was soon adopted throughout France and later in other countries, primarily in Germany and Austria. It is characterized by elegance, and an excessive use of curves in ornamentation. The word Rococo is derived from the French word *rocaille,* which denoted a shell-covered rock.

By the end of the Baroque, the Rococo had replaced the complex, exaggerated forms with elegance and extreme decoration. It portrayed how the upper class became more alienated, more detached from common people as the elite displayed their wealth through art, particularly under the reign of King Louis XV. The Rococo, an abbreviated period, spanned the latter part of the Baroque and early Classic periods.

Harpsichord - A popular keyboard instrument of the Baroque and Classic periods; its strings were plucked by a small plectrum or quill.

François Couperin (1668-1733) was a French Baroque composer, organist, and harpsichordist. He is best remembered for his keyboard pieces in the Rococo style.

Suggested Search:
   Le Tic-toc Choc ou les Maillotins (18e Ordre)
   joryvinikour

II.   Emfindsam stil (sensitive style)
      An emotional style of music associated with the Rococo
style practiced by the German middle class of the late 18th
century, with less emphasis on elegance. Emfindsam stil
attempted to express various emotions throughout the piece
by sudden harmonic shifts and changes of mood. Frequently
referred to as *emfindsamkeit* (sensitivity).

         Carl Philipp Emanuel Bach (1714-1788) was a
         German Classic period musician and composer, the
         second son of J.S. Bach. He composed over 900
         works; he is best known for his harpsichord works in
         the Empfindsam stil.

III. Terms
      A. Form - The design and organization of a composer's
         work.

      B. Movement - A section of a complete work with its
         own form but conceived as part of a whole
         composition, such as a symphony with four
         movements.

      C. Crescendo - A gradual increase in the volume of
         sound.

      D. Diminuendo, decrescendo - A gradual decrease in the
         volume of sound.

      E. Orchestra - An ensemble of strings, winds, brass, and
         percussion instruments, with more than one player to
         a part.

IV.   Symphony - A large work for orchestra, usually consisting of
      four movements.

NOTE: An orchestra is a group of instruments; a symphony is what the orchestra plays.

During the Classic Period, the Industrial Revolution (1760-1840) brought new manufacturing processes throughout Europe. These new processes, including iron production, led to stronger metals and materials; also, hand production changed to machine production. Since instruments were constructed of stronger materials and could be constructed faster, they were more reliable and more available. Among all genres of music during the Classic period, the symphony received the greatest attention.

A. Typical movements of a Classic symphony

    1.   First movement: Sonata-allegro - The form generally used as the first movement in symphonies, string quartets and sonatas during the Classic period and early Romantic period. It eventually became known as sonata form. It consisted of Exposition, Development, Recapitulation, Coda.

        a. Exposition - In sonata-allegro form, the first section in which the themes are introduced.

        b. Development - In sonata-allegro form, the second section after the Exposition, which presents the themes in various keys.

        c. Recapitulation - In sonata-allegro form, the third section restates the themes introduced in the Exposition.

        d. Coda - A concluding section of a symphony following the

Recapitulation section of sonata-allegro form.

Suggested Search:
Wolfgang Amadeus Mozart –
Symphony No. 40, G minor, KV 550 –
1st

2.   Second movement: Theme and variations - Form in which a musical idea or theme recurs but is varied each time in rhythm, harmony, or some other feature of the music; usually, the 2nd movement of a Classic symphony.

Suggested Search:
Mozart, "Ah! vous dirai je maman" Twinkle Twinkle, Little Star KV 265

3.   Third movement: Minuet and Trio - A form based on two dances that consists of three parts, A B A (minuet, trio, minuet); usually, the 3rd movement of a Classic symphony.

4.   Fourth movement: Rondo - A musical form in which the first section recurs multiple times between alternating sections; a schematic for rondo is A B A C A D A or A B A C A B A; usually the 4th movement of a Classic symphony.

Suggested Search:
Mozart - *Flute Concerto No.2 In D Major*
Mozart K.314 Third Movement – Allegro

V.   Concerto, solo concerto (See Chapter III)

VI.   Chamber music - Music for a small group that is performed in a home or small auditorium, with one player to a part. It is considered intimate music suited to subtle nuances. The most popular form of chamber music during the Classic period was the string quartet.

   A. String quartet - An instrumental ensemble for chamber music which consists of Violin I, Violin II, Viola, and Cello; also, a genre of music consisting of three or four movements arranged for this ensemble.

Suggested Search:
   Wedding String Quartet - Canon in D (Best Version) (Johann Pachelbel)

   Tale As Old As Time from the movie Beauty And The Beast - Wedding String Quartet

VII.   Patronage system - During the Classic period, many musicians worked under what is known as the patronage system. Musicians and/or composers would work as servants to powerful and wealthy nobility writing and performing pieces for their patron.

   A. Esterházy Family
      Esterházy is a Hungarian noble family which dates to the Middle Ages. Since the 17th century, this family was among the great landowners of the Kingdom of Hungary.

      Prince Nikolaus Esterházy built a palace known as the Esterháza Palace located near the border of Hungary and Austria, which is sometimes called the "Hungarian Versailles." The Esterháza palace had 126 guest rooms, two opera houses, a theater that could seat 400 guests, a concert hall, and a chapel.

      Guests at Esterháza came from all over Europe and spent three or four days of entertainment: fox hunting, fishing, playing sports, attending concerts, and relaxing.

Suggested Search:
> Esterházy Palace From Above - Drone Footage
>
> The Haydn Concert Hall in the Esterhazy Palace, Eisenstadt

B. Franz Josef Haydn (1732-1809)

Franz Josef Haydn was an Austrian composer of the Classic period and was instrumental in the development of the symphony and chamber music such as the string quartet. He composed over 104 symphonies and 68 string quartets. His contributions to musical form have earned him the title "Father of the symphony."

Haydn spent 28 years of his career as a court musician for the wealthy Esterházy family at their remote estate near the Hungarian border. Haydn's contract at Esterháza required him to compose whatever the family demanded, chamber music, symphonies, opera, and sacred music. He also supervised and trained all musicians, which included 25-35 singers and instrumentalists. During much of his career he was the most celebrated composer in Europe.

Suggested Search:
> Haydn String Quartet No. 62, Op. 76 No. 3 "Emperor" (2nd mov) Veridis Quartet (Live performance)

Suggested Search:
> Haydn, Symphony No. 94 in G Major (Surprise) Second Movement: Andante
>
> Haydn: "Farewell" Symphony #45, IV. Finale | New Century Chamber Orchestra

Hob, Hoboken - Abbreviation for Anthony Hoboken, who compiled a catalogue of the musical compositions by Joseph Haydn. Works by Haydn are often indicated using their Hoboken catalogue number, rather than opus.

ANECDOTE:
Franz Joseph Haydn died in Vienna in 1809 when Austria was at war with Napoleon. Because Vienna was occupied by Napoleon's troops, Haydn's funeral was simple, and he was buried in his home parish in Vienna. After his burial, two men bribed the gravedigger to open the grave so they could steal the composer's head. Their act was motivated by a scientific interest in discovering whether a person's mental capacity was associated with the size of the skull. Haydn's skull passed through several hands during the years until 1954, when it was transferred to its final resting place, completing the 145-year-long burial process.

C.   Wolfgang Amadeus Mozart
Mozart, born in Salzburg, Austria, showed exceptional ability on keyboard and violin at an exceedingly early age; he composed his first piece at the age of five and performed before European royalty. He composed more than 600 works, symphonies, chamber music, operas, and choral music. He is among the most popular of Classic composers, and his influence on Western music is significant.
During Mozart's final years in Vienna, he composed many of his best-known symphonies, concertos, and operas, and portions of the Requiem, which was unfinished at the time of his death. K. is an abbreviation for Ludwig von Köchel, who compiled a catalog of W.A. Mozart's works.

Suggested Search:
Top 10 Mozart Songs

Amadeus Clip
(The above excerpt is taken from the movie "Amadeus" 1984).

Mozart "Eine kleine Nachtmusik" I. Allegro

VIII.   Vocal Music

   A. Comic opera - Comic opera is a sung dramatic work of a light or comic nature, usually with spoken dialogue and written in the vernacular.

    1.   Types of comic opera

      a. Ballad opera - Genre of 18th-century comic plays popular in England and Ireland featuring songs in English. The texts were usually satirical poking fun at English political or social life and Italian opera, immensely popular in London at that time (Chapter III).

      b. Opera comique - In the 18th century, a light French comic opera, which used spoken dialogue; in the 19th century, could be either comic or tragic.

      c. Singspiel - Genre of German light opera, which consists of songs, spoken dialogue, choruses and instrumental music.

      d. Opera buffa - Italian comic opera of the 18th century; sung throughout; the most popular form of comic opera.

          a. Intermezzo - Genre of Italian comic opera performed between the acts of a serious opera; forerunner of opera buffa.

   b. Pants role or trousers role - A male role, usually for an adolescent, performed by a female singer.

   c. Ensemble finale - The final scene of an opera or musical in which the principal singers return to the stage and sing simultaneously with different words and music.

   e. *The Marriage of Figaro*, by Wolfgang Amadeus Mozart, is a well-known and popular opera buffa.

Suggested Search:
    "Cinque, Dieci, Venti" - Alison Hagley and Gerald Finley (1994)

    "Voi Che Sapete" (English Subtitles)

    "Gente Gente All'armi All'armi" / Finale

B. Sacred Music

Among the principal genres of sacred music during the Classic period are masses, oratorios, motets, and other incidental pieces composed for the Church. Both Franz Josef Haydn and Wolfgang Amadeus Mozart composed sacred music.

Haydn composed six masses that were designed more for concert performance than for use in church. He composed three oratorios; *The Creation* and *The Seasons* are the only two that are regularly performed and enjoyed by today's audiences. Many believe that *The Creation* is second in popularity only to *Messiah* by G. F. Handel.

Suggested Search:
   F.J. Haydn - "The heavens are telling" ⟨The Creation⟩ Oratorio / Christopher Hogwood

Mozart composed masses, oratorios, as well as smaller forms of motets and other works for the Church. *Ave verum corpus* is a work that Mozart composed in the final year of his life. It was written to be performed on the *Feast of Corpus Christi*. Mozart wrote the words *sotto voce* (meaning 'very softly, in a subdued manner') on the score to be sung throughout.

Suggested Search:
   Wolfgang Amadeus Mozart - *Ave Verum Corpus*

Mozart's *Requiem Mass in D Minor* was left unfinished at his death; it was completed by one of his students. His *Requiem Mass* (Mass for the Dead) was his last composition on a grand scale and is considered a masterpiece of the Classic period.

Suggested Search:
   Mozart *Requiem* Bernstein 03. Dies irae.mpg

Among the composers of the Classic period, many scholars believe only Haydn and Mozart composed works that became classics. They both attained international fame and are considered the epitome of the Classic tradition.

Chapter V Age of Romanticism, 1825-1900

Chapter V, "Age of Romanticism, 1825-1900" will help the student understand the differences between the Classic and Romantic periods. Prominent composers of this period are presented along with their compositions representing different genres. The student will be introduced to unfamiliar terms such as art song, absolute vs. program music, rubato, leitmotif, and verismo.

The Romantic Period was marked by a time of expansion, mystery, and emotion. Romantic composers broke away from time-honored forms and emphasized freedom of expression; they began to allow feelings to replace reason. Composers were concerned about what later generations would think of them. Their works were considered an extension of themselves as their music reflected the emotions of their lives. Society in general was intrigued by unknown, faraway, exotic places. Some of the favorite subjects were love of nature, witches, the spirit world, and mythology.

The root of the word "Romantic" can be traced back to folklore and stories of the Medieval Period, which were called "Romanz," pronounced Ro-MANZ. The Medieval Romanz became a favorite subject matter for artists, composers, and writers; hence, the name Romantic. The Medieval Romanz usually dealt with the deeds and adventures of a knight, or hero rescuing a "damsel in distress."

For the first time, many educational institutions included music in the curriculum and for the first time, music became a very lucrative business. Virtuosos found themselves in great demand. Due to the Industrial Revolution, now throughout most of Europe, musical instruments became more durable, reliable, and less expensive, which made them more accessible to a rising middle class.

According to several scholars, the piano, with its double-stop action, sustaining pedal, and cast-iron frame, became a symbol of the Romantic period. Piano music was one of the most important developments of this time, surpassing the interest in composing for the orchestra.

Historically, women in the arts, particularly in music, were considered untalented and sometimes unwelcome. Now compositions of previous centuries are being heard again, and female composers are being accepted, such as Fanny Mendelssohn Hensel and Clara Schumann.

Some of the most influential composers during this period were: Ludwig van Beethoven, Franz Schubert, Felix Mendelssohn Bartholdy, Johannes Brahms, Piotr Ilyich Tchaikovsky, Frédéric Chopin, Franz Liszt, Robert Schumann, Georges Bizet, Giuseppe Verdi, Giacomo Puccini, and Richard Wagner.

I.   New Types of music in the Romantic period.

    A. Absolute music - Instrumental music that contains no association with a program, story, or poem of any kind. Example: *Symphony No. 5 in C Minor.*

    B. Program music - Instrumental music that tells a story or relates to an event; music that is intended to evoke images usually listed in a printed program. Example: *Romeo and Juliet.*

    C. The art song, a composition for solo voice and piano, is unique to the Romantic period and is one of the most distinctive forms of music during this era. The piano part is not merely accompaniment; it plays an integral part in the song and helps the solo voice interpret the text. The piano might suggest "a galloping horse" or "spinning wheel." Many art song texts were poems by famous German poets of the Romantic period, such as Heinrich Heine, Johann von Göthe, and Wilhelm Müller. Art song (German: *lied*, singular; *lieder*, plural) brief definition: A song in which the piano accompaniment, poetic text and melody are of equal importance, usually through composed, although some may be strophic, and requiring high standards of performance.

Transition from Classic period to Romantic period

II.   Ludwig van Beethoven, (1770-1827) transitional composer.
      Ludwig van Beethoven, recognized as one of the most
celebrated and influential of all composers, was a German
composer and pianist. He was an important figure in the
transition between the Classic and Romantic periods; he was
one of the first composers to successfully live apart from the
patronage system. Beethoven was afflicted with an ear
disease in his early twenties which led to complete deafness
by the last decade of his life. On a retreat to Heiligenstadt,
just outside Vienna, he wrote: "I would have ended my life –
it was only my art that held me back. . . it seemed to me
impossible to leave the world until I had brought forth all that
I felt was within me." ("Beethoven: Compositions,
biography, siblings and more facts") This letter, written to his
brothers in 1802, is known as the *Heiligenstadt Testament*
and was published in 1828. He composed nine symphonies,
along with numerous string quartets, sonatas, concertos, one
mass and one opera.

Heiligenstadt testament -A letter written by Beethoven to his
brothers to come to terms with his deafness; considered to be
like a last will and testament.

Suggested Search:
          "Pathétique" *Sonata No. 8 in C Minor* Op. 13, 1st
          Movement
          Barenboim plays Beethoven "Pathétique" Sonata No.
          8 in C Minor Op. 13, 1st Mov.

          Immortal Beloved Deaf Scene, "Moonlight Sonata"

          The above excerpt is from the movie "Immortal
      Beloved" (1994) which chronicles Beethoven's
      struggle with his loss of hearing.

      Sonata No. 14 "Moonlight"
      Beethoven Sonata N° 14 'moonlight' Daniel
      Barenboim

          Symphony No. 5, C Minor, 1st Movement.

Symphony No. 5, in C Minor is perhaps the best-known of Beethoven's nine symphonies, particularly the 1st movement. The theme is based upon a rhythmic idea of four notes: three short notes, one long note.

Suggested Search:

Beethoven: Symphony No. 5, 1st movement | Paavo Järvi and the Deutsche Kammerphilharmonie Bremen

Symphony No. 9, D Minor, Opus 125 4th Movement.

The 4th movement of *Symphony No. 9* is acclaimed as one of Beethoven's most famous works.

This movement includes a setting of the poem "Ode to Joy" by Friedrich von Schiller, a German poet, philosopher, and playwright. The text expresses a desire for universal brotherhood. The Protestant hymn called "Joyful, Joyful We Adore Thee" by Henry van Dyke is a poem written with the intention of setting it to the melody of this 4th movement.

Suggested Search:
Symphony No. 9 "CHORAL"
Beethoven: Symphony No. 9 / Karajan · Berliner Philharmoniker

III.   Other Romantic Composers

A. Franz Schubert (1797-1828)
Franz Schubert, an Austrian composer, spent most of his life in Vienna. He died before his 32nd birthday but was extremely prolific during his lifetime.

Schubert's compositional output consists of over 600 secular art songs (*lieder*), eight complete symphonies (another remained unfinished), sacred music, and piano music. Schubert was not widely recognized during his lifetime, but interest in his work increased significantly in the years following his death. Schubert, a transitional composer, is listed among the greatest composers of the late Classic and early Romantic eras.

Suggested Search:
> *Der Erl König* (The Erlking)
> Schubert_ Der Erlkönig (D328) - subtitled in English
>
> *The Erlking* sand art
> Erlking sand art with subtitles
>
> *Heidenröslein* (A Wild Rose)
> Heidenroeslein
>
> *Gretchen am Spinnrade* (Gretchen at the Spinning Wheel)
> Schubert: Gretchen am spinnrade", op.2, D.118 - Te Kanawa

ANECDOTE:
Schubert was among the 20,000 mourners who lined the streets of Vienna at Beethoven's funeral procession. After the ceremony at the cemetery, Schubert and some friends went to a local tavern to have a drink.

Schubert lifted his glass and offered a toast 'to him who will go next!' Twenty months later, Schubert died at age of 31; he was next.

B. Felix Mendelssohn (1809-1847)

Felix Mendelssohn Bartholdy, German composer during the Romantic period, stands out among other musicians because of the fortunate circumstances into which he was born; he was born into wealth. Mendelssohn was the son of a wealthy, aristocratic family. He was accepted into the finest social circles and led a life free from the stresses of many composers his age. He was also skilled as pianist, organist, and conductor. Mendelssohn was recognized early as a musical prodigy.

Mendelssohn enjoyed early success in Germany, where he also revived interest in the music of J.S. Bach by discovering and performing a forgotten manuscript of Bach's *Passion According to St. Matthew*.

Mendelssohn wrote symphonies, concertos, oratorios, piano music, and chamber music. His best-known and most popular work is his *A Midsummer Night's Dream*. Mendelssohn composed two oratorios: *St. Paul* and *Elijah*. His *Songs Without Words* are his most famous solo piano compositions. He is among the most popular composers of the **Romantic** period.

Suggested Search:

A Midsummer Night's Dream Overture Op. 21 Mendelssohn - A Midsummer Night's Dream Overture, Op. 21 (Kurt Masur, Gewandhausorchestra)

St. Paul "How Lovely are the Messengers" - 2015 CMEA Central Coast Section (CCS) High School Honor Choir

Elijah "Ye People Rend Your Hearts/If with all your Hearts"

Elijah- Ye People Rend Your Hearts/If with all your Hearts- Ethan Bremner

Song Without Words Op. 53 No. 1
Mendelssohn - Song Without Words Op. 53 No. 1

ANECDOTE:
When Mendelsohn conducted the first performance of Bach's *Passion According to St. Matthew*, he stepped to the podium and discovered that someone had mistakenly placed the wrong score on the stand. Without the audience or performers being aware, he conducted the entire work from memory, even turning pages at the appropriate time.

C. Fanny Mendelssohn (1805-1847)
Fanny Mendelssohn Hensel (sister of Felix) composed over 450 compositions. Most of her works disappeared from public awareness after her death until late in the 20th century. Like her brother, Fanny was a child prodigy with perfect pitch. She performed 24 **preludes** from J.S. Bach's *Well-Tempered Clavier* from memory for her father when she was fourteen.

Many of her songs were published under Felix's name while most of her remaining works exist only in manuscript.

Suggested Search:
 Die Mainacht - Fanny Mendelssohn Hensel

 Fantasie in g-moll for Cello
 Fanny Mendelssohn, Fantasie in g-moll for Cello and Piano (1829)

D. Johannes Brahms (1833-1897)

Johannes Brahms, German composer and pianist of the Romantic period, spent much of his professional life in Vienna, Austria. His reputation as a composer grouped him with J.S. Bach and Ludwig van Beethoven as one of the "Three Bs" of music. Brahms composed for symphony orchestra, piano, voice, and chorus. Brahms was extremely critical of himself as a composer and destroyed many of his works and left others unpublished. Brahms, a virtuoso pianist, premiered many of his own works.

Suggested Search:
> *Brahms' Lullaby*
> Yo-Yo Ma, Kathryn Stott - Lullaby (Brahms)
>
> *Symphony No. 3, F Major*
> Brahms: Symphony No. 3 / Rattle · Berliner Philharmoniker

Ein Deutsche Requiem (A German Requiem) is a large-scale work for orchestra, chorus, and a soprano and baritone soloist. The fourth movement, "How Lovely is Thy Dwelling Place," is the highpoint for many listeners.

Suggested Search:
> *How Lovely Is Thy Dwelling Place*, with Organ | The Tabernacle Choir

E. Peter Ilyich Tchaikovsky (1840-1893)
Peter Ilyich Tchaikovsky lived during the Romantic period and was the first Russian composer whose music made an impression internationally; he is widely acclaimed as the most popular Russian composer in music history.

Tchaikovsky is recognized as having contributed some of the most popular compositions in the classical repertoire. His works include the popular ballets *The Nutcracker, Swan Lake* and *The Sleeping Beauty* and the concert overture, *The 1812 Overture*.

Suggested Search:
> *The Nutcracker* (Suite)
>> "Dance of the Sugar Plum Fairy"
>> Pyotr Ilyich Tchaikovsky / Anna Nikulina - Dance of the Sugar Plum Fairy / 2014

> *Swan Lake*
>> "Dance of the Little Swans"
>> Swan Lake, Tchaikovsky - Dance of the Little Swans Medici.TV

> *Sleeping Beauty*
>> Tchaikovsky - Sleeping Beauty - Ballet Medici.TV

The 1812 Overture, is program music written in 1880 by Tchaikovsky to commemorate Russia's successful defense against Napoleon's invading army in 1812. The overture was premiered in Moscow on August 20, 1882, to inaugurate the Cathedral of Christ the Redeemer, which also memorialized the 1812 defeat of Napoleon. Tchaikovsky hated this *The 1812 Overture;* he considered it very loud and noisy and without value." Ironically, he is best remembered for *The 1812 Overture* and the victory of Russia over Napoleon in 1812.

Suggested Search:
1812 Overture
Tchaikovsky : Overture 1812 (Full, Choral) (Sure, best version ever) - Ashkenazy*

ANECDOTE:
When Boston Pops conductor Arthur Fiedler decided to include the *1812 Overture* as part of his 1974 Independence Day performance, he programed fireworks, live cannons, and a steeple bell choir.

Since then, orchestras all over the United States began to perform it and the *1812 Overture* is now commonly performed during Independence Day celebrations. As a result, many Americans have come to believe that the piece represents the victory of the United States against the British Empire during the War of 1812.

F. Niccolò Paganini (1782-1840)
Niccolò Paganini, was an Italian violinist and composer during the Romantic period and was the most renowned violin virtuoso of his time. He became a popular idol and was considered one of the first "personality" performers. He enhanced the Romantic mystique of the virtuoso and revolutionized violin technique. His composition entitled *24 Caprices for Solo Violin Op. 1* has challenged many violinists and has been an inspiration for many composers and performers.

Suggested Search:
Caprice No. 24 In A Minor
Niccolò Paganini: Caprice No. 24 In A Minor

"Paganini, the Devil's Violinist"

David Garrett (Niccolò Paganini) Caprice 24
[The Devil's Violinist]

The above excerpt is from the movie "The Devil's Violinist" (2015), a film based on the life story of Italian violinist and composer Niccolò Paganini.

G. Frédéric Chopin (1810-1849)
Frédéric Chopin, recognized as "The Poet of the Piano," was a Polish composer and virtuoso pianist of the Romantic period who wrote primarily for the solo piano. Over 230 works of Chopin survive; however, many compositions have been lost. Most of his well-known works involve the solo piano; the rest of his works are either piano concertos, art songs or chamber music.

Rubato - (Italian, "robbed") A piano technique common during the Romantic period in which the right hand holds back ("robs") and then hurries along ("pays back") the tempo, while the left hand maintains a strict tempo. Done for expressive purposes, this technique typified the piano performances of Frédéric Chopin.

Suggested Search:
Nocturne Op. 9 No. 2
Yundi Li plays Chopin Nocturne Op. 9 No. 2 in E flat Major Piano

Prelude in E Minor (op.28 no. 4)
Eric Lu – Prelude in E minor Op. 28 No. 4 (Prize-winners' Concert)

H. Franz Liszt (1811-1886)
Hungarian composer Franz Liszt was one of the most flamboyant musical personalities of the Romantic period.

After attending a charity concert for the victims of a cholera epidemic organized by Niccolò Paganini, Liszt was determined to become as great a virtuoso on the piano as Paganini was on the violin.

Liszt was the first performer to turn the piano sideways so the audience could see his profile when he performed; prior to this, pianists performed with their backs toward the audience. He was also the first to perform an entire recital from memory. As a young man, Liszt enjoyed the kind of popularity experienced by today's rock stars.

> *Suggested Search*:
> *Liebestraum*
> Lang Lang: Franz Liszt – "Love Dream" (Liebestraum), S. 541 No. 3
>
> *La Campanella*
> Lang Lang Franz Liszt - La Campanella 2012

ANECDOTE:

A young maiden in the court of Saxe-Weimar in Central Germany had an unusual fragrance that puzzled her friends; she continually reeked of stale tobacco. Later, she confessed that she had picked up an old cigar that Liszt had discarded in the street. Devotedly, she picked it up and enclosed it in an expensive locket that she wore around her neck.

I. Robert Schuman (1810-1856)

According to many musicologists, the German Robert Schumann exemplified the true Romantic ideal; he was composer, author, and music critic. He founded *Die Neue Zeitschrift für Musik* (The New Journal of Music) which promoted and praised young musicians while he attacked others whom he felt were inferior.

Schumann is widely regarded as one of the greatest composers of the Romantic period. In his early career, he was recognized as a virtuoso pianist, but an injury to his right hand ended this dream. Schumann then focused his musical energies on composing.

Schumann composed works for piano and orchestra, many art songs (*lieder*), four symphonies, and chamber works. In 1840, Schumann married Friedrich Wieck's daughter, Clara, against the wishes of her father, and following a long legal battle. Clara also composed music and had a successful concert career as a pianist.

Schumann suffered from severe depression and, after a suicide attempt in 1854, he was admitted to a mental asylum. He died two years later in 1856 without having recovered from his mental illness.

Alter personalities of Robert Schumann
1. Florestan - impulsive, tempestuous
2. Eusebius - mild, meek, dreamy
3. Mr. Raro – mediator

Dichterliebe - "A Poet's Love" - a song cycle by Robert Schumann consisting of 16 settings of poems by Heinrich Heine. Schumann composed *Dichterliebe* in 1840 after he married Clara. The entire year of 1840 was dedicated to writing songs for Clara and is commonly referred to as "The Year of Song."

Suggested Search:
  Dichterliebe

Francisco Araiza: Robert Schumann - Im wunderschönen Monat Mai (song cycle "Dichterliebe")

Francisco Araiza: Robert Schumann -
Ein Jüngling liebt ein Mädchen
(Dichterliebe-Liederzyklus)

Francisco Araiza: Robert Schumann -
Ich grolle nicht (Dichterliebe-
Liederzyklus)

Cello Concerto in A Minor
Schumann Cello Concerto op 129 | Kian
Soltani | Christoph Eschenbach | SWR
Symphonieorchester | HD

Suggested Search:
  Träumerei
  Vladimir Horowitz - Träumerei - Schumann
  (Kinderszenen)

J. Clara Wieck Schumann (1819-1896)
    Clara Wieck Schumann was one of the most
distinguished pianists of the Romantic period. Her
husband was the composer, Robert Schumann.
    Robert moved into the Wieck household and
became a piano student of Clara's father, Friedrich;
she was only 11 and he was 20.

    When Clara was 18, Robert proposed to her, and
she accepted. Wieck opposed the marriage, as he did
not much approve of Robert and did not give his
permission. Robert and Clara went to court and the
judge's decision was to allow them to marry. In 1840,
Clara and Robert were married.

Suggested Search:
  Three romances for violin and piano Op 22
  Clara-Jumi Kang: C. Schumann, Three
  Romances for violin and piano, Op. 22

Liebst du um Schönheit
Hélène Grimaud & Anne Sofie von Otter -
Liebst du um Schönheit

IV.   Composers of Dramatic Music of the Romantic period

A. Georges Bizet (1838-1875)
Georges Bizet spent most of his life in Paris,
France, and was primarily an opera composer during
the Romantic period; his career was cut short by his
early death at age 38. Bizet was little known and
achieved few successes before his opera, *Carmen*,
which has become one of the most popular works in
the entire opera repertoire. Bizet's fame rests entirely
on this one work, *Carmen*.

The opera *Carmen*, set in Spain, infuriated many at
its premiere, but has since become one of the most
popular operas of all time. Some were outraged that a
"murder" could be performed on stage (final scene),
rather than off stage.

Suggested Search:
Carmen: "L'amour est un oiseau rebelle"
Habanera (Elina Garanca)

"Votre Toast"
Carmen (opera), Act II: "Votre Toast
(Toreador Song)"

Carmen:
Carmen: Final Scene (Elina Garanca, Roberto
Alagna)

B. Giuseppe Verdi (1813-1901)
The name Giuseppe Verdi is synonymous with
Italian opera. Verdi came to dominate the Italian
opera scene and became one of the greatest opera
composers in history.

In his early operas Verdi was sympathetic with the Risorgimento (Resurgence or revival) movement which sought the unification of Italy. He sided with the Nationalist Green (Verdi) Party and allowed his name to be used to further their cause. Due to his popularity among the people, he also participated briefly as an elected politician. His operas remain extremely popular, especially *Rigoletto*, *Il trovatore* and *La traviata*.

<u>V</u>ittorio <u>E</u>mmanuel <u>Ré</u> <u>D</u>'´Italia - "<u>V-e-r-d-i</u>"

During the Austrian occupation of Northern Italy, the patriotic cry "Viva Verdi" also stood for the popular slogan, Vittorio Emmanuele, Re D' Italia (Victor Emmanuel, King of Italy).

Suggested Search:
> *Rigoletto*
>> 'La donna è mobile' (Verdi; Vittorio Grigòlo, The Royal Opera)

La Traviata
> 'Brindisi' ('The Drinking Song') – Glyndebourne

Il Trovatore
> "Anvil chorus" (Chorus of the Hungarian State Opera House)

C. Richard Wagner (1813-1883)
Richard Wagner, German, is best known for creating several complex operas, including *Tristan und Isolde* and *Der Ring des Nibelungen,* commonly referred to as the "Ring Cycle." He is also as well known for his antisemitic writings, which made him a favorite of Adolf Hitler.

Wagner considered himself a composer, an author, a philosopher, and an architect. He was one of the first German composers to write operas in German; he preferred to call his operas "music dramas."

Wagner designed and constructed a theater that was dedicated to the performance of his own colossal presentations, the Bayreuth Theater. He located the orchestra in a pit a little lower than the stage so the audience would have an unobstructed view of the singers on stage; this has become the custom in opera theaters today.

In many of Wagner's writings, the concept of *Gesamtkunstwerk*, the union of all the arts, became the central focus, which became the basis for his compositions; the visual arts and aural arts were of equal importance. In addition to *Tristan und Isolde* and the "Ring Cycle," some of his other famous works are *The Flying Dutchman, Tannhäuser*, and *Lohengrin*.

Gesamtkunstwerk - "Union of the Arts." A German term used by Richard Wagner in his music dramas in which music, acting, dance, staging, and scenic designs are all merged into one production.

Leitmotif - A compositional device in which a recurring melodic or harmonic fragment is associated with a person, event, mood, or object; used primarily by Richard Wagner in his music dramas.

Bayreuth theater - An opera house in Bayreuth, Germany, designed and constructed by Richard Wagner for the exclusive performances of his music dramas.

Suggested Search: The Bayreuther Festspielhaus: Auditorium

Operas (Music dramas)

Der Ring des Nibelungen ("Ring Cycle").
The "Ring Cycle" consists of four operas
designed to be performed on consecutive
days. The total length of the "Ring Cycle" is
approximately 15 hours.

Suggested Search:
First opera: *Das Rheingold*

Second opera:
Die Walküre
Metropolitan Opera Orchestra –
Wagner: Ride of the Valkyries - Ring
(Official Video)

Third opera: *Siegfried*

Fourth opera: *Götterdämmerung*

Suggested Search:
The Flying Dutchman The Flying Dutchman 7
Minute Highlights - San Francisco Opera
(2013)

Lohengrin Richard Wagner: Lohengrin -
Vorspiel 3. Akt und "Wedding March"

ANECDOTE:
On one occasion a friend of Gioachino Rossini
(1792-1868), asked him what he thought of
Wagner's opera, *Tristan und Isolde*. "Ah, it is a
beautiful work, such grace, such power over our
old dramatic scores – including my own," replied
Rossini. The friend came closer and noticed that
Rossini was reading Wagner's score upside down.

D. Giacomo Puccini (1858-1924)

The last great opera composer during the Romantic era was Giacomo Puccini. He has been called "the greatest composer of Italian opera after Verdi." He developed his works in the verismo style, of which he became one of its leading proponents. Puccini's most renowned works are *La bohème, Tosca*, and *Madama Butterfly*, all of which are among the standard opera repertoires.

Puccini's final opera was *Turandot* which contains one of the most famous arias of opera, "Nessun dorma." *Gianni Schicchi*, is Puccini's only comic opera. It contains the well-known soprano aria, "O mio babbino caro."

Verismo is a style that depicts real life and real situations in 19th -century opera; it is associated with opera composers such as Giacomo Puccini and Giuseppe Verdi.

Suggested Search:
La Bohéme
"Si. Mi chiamano Mimi" (Angela Gheorghiu)

"Che gelida manina" La Boheme - Che Gelida Manina - José Carreras as Rodolpho

Madama Butterfly
Un bel di vedremo - Puccini's Madame Butterfly Huang Ying

Turandot
Nessun Dorma - Marcello Giordani - Live At Met 2009

TURANDOT - Puccini - Final: Padre augusto
conosco il nome dello straniero! Placido Domingo
1988

Gianni Schicchi
Nino Machaidze - "O mio babbino caro" - Gianni
Schicchi La Scala '08

V.   Romantic composers in America

  A. John Phillip Sousa (1854-1932)
      John Phillip Sousa, famous primarily for American
  military and patriotic marches, was an American
  composer of the late Romantic period; he is known as
  "The March King." Among his best-known marches
  are *The Stars and Stripes Forever* and *Semper Fidelis*
  (Official March of the United States Marine Corps)

      Suggested Search:
        The Stars and Stripes Forever
        U.S. Marine Band United States Marine Band

        Washington Post March
        U.S. Marine Band United States Marine Band

        Semper Fidelis
        U.S. Marine Band United States Marine Band

  B. Stephen Collins Foster (1826-1864)
      Stephen Collins Foster is recognized by many as
  "the father of American music." He was an American
  songwriter primarily known for his parlor and
  minstrel music. Foster wrote over 200 songs; among
  his best-known are "Oh! Susanna," "My Old
  Kentucky Home," "Jeannie with the Light Brown
  Hair," and "Beautiful Dreamer." He has been
  identified as "the most famous American songwriter
  of the nineteenth century" and may be the most
  recognizable American composer in other countries.

Suggested Search:
Oh! Susanna
"Confederate Song"

My Old Kentucky Home

I Dream of Jeannie with the Light Brown Hair

Beautiful Dreamer

C. Louis Moreau Gottschalk (1829-1869)
Louis Moreau Gottschalk became the first American composer and pianist to enjoy an international reputation, particularly in Europe. He is best known as a virtuoso performer of his own piano works. He was born in New Orleans, Louisiana, but spent most of his working career outside of the United States, particularly in South America and Caribbean countries. Although born and reared in New Orleans, he was a supporter of the Union cause during the American Civil War. Early pieces like *The Banjo* were based on Gottschalk's memories of the music he heard growing up in New Orleans.

Suggested Search: "The Banjo by L.M. Gottschalk"

VI.   Composers of Operetta during Romantic Period

Patter songs - A patter song is a setting of humorous words sung very rapidly; they are typically found in operettas.

A. William S. Gilbert (1836-1911) and Arthur Sullivan (1871-1896)
"Gilbert and Sullivan" refers to the theatrical partnership of William S. Gilbert (lyricist) and Arthur Sullivan (composer).

They collaborated on 14 comic operas, of which *The Pirates of Penzance, H.M.S. Pinafore, The Mikado,* and *Iolanthe* are among the best known. Gilbert, who wrote the words, created imaginative situations in these operas where each is filled with absurdity. Sullivan composed melodies that could convey both humor and silliness.

Suggested Search:
> *Pirates of Penzance*
>> "I Am the Very Model of a Modern Major General"

> *H.M.S. Pinafore*
>> "I Am the Captain of the Pinafore"
> *The Mikado*
>> "Three Little Maids from School Are We"

B. Victor Herbert (1859-1924) Victor Herbert was born in Dublin, Ireland but spent much of his life in Stuttgart, Germany, where he received his education. He moved to the United States with his wife where he became a composer of operettas and light musicals. He produced two operas, 43 operettas and various compositions for orchestra and band.

Suggested Search: Victor Herbert *Babes in Toyland,* "March of the toys

Chapter VI Music in the 20ᵗʰ Century and Later

In Chapter VI, "Music in the 20ᵗʰ Century and Later," the student will be introduced to various sub-movements of the 20th century: Impressionism, Expressionism, Primitivism, and Experimentalism. Significant composers from each group will be presented along with selections of their compositions. The following terms associated with these sub-movements include Sprechstimme, Sprechgesang, atonality, serialism, twelve-tone technique, polytonality, aleatory music, and prepared piano.

By the beginning of the 20ᵗʰ century, music continued in the late Romantic period style, dominated by the Germanic tradition. However, composers began to push the bounds of traditional music to break away from the traditions of the Romantic period. Composers believed that every combination of notes possible, rhythmically and melodically, had been exhausted over the course of centuries.

The Impressionist movement (Impressionism), led by Claude Debussy, was being developed in France. In Vienna, Arnold Schönberg, influenced by the Expressionist movement (Expressionism) that arose in the early part of the 20th century, developed atonality; in this system, he eliminated the tonal center and developed a technique called twelve-tone technique. Igor Stravinsky, a Russian who escaped to Paris in the early 1900's, was particularly drawn to the short-lived movement Primitivism in his early career.

In the early 20ᵗʰ century, a revolutionary approach to music resulted in a group of American composers called Experimentalists (Experimentalism). They extended the boundaries of music to include sounds (including the human voice) that were not necessarily pleasant nor desirable. Microtones, intervals that are smaller than a semitone, were introduced into the musical vocabulary.

The term electronic music was used later to include all forms of music involving computers, synthesizers, multimedia, and other electronic devices. Another new term, aleatory music (chance music), describes works that produce unpredictable sounds and results. In the genre of Experimental Music are the compositions of Charles Ives, John Cage, Pauline Oliveros, and Henry Cowell, along with others.

By the early 1920's-30's, a generation of American composers successfully devoted their professional lives to composing music. They are sometimes called "American Nationalists." They found traditional tonality more palatable to their tastes, as well as that of the American public. Aaron Copland and George Gershwin are among the most well-known as they opened the door to a new genre of music: musicals.

William Grant Still was the first African American to gain international recognition as a composer. His *Afro-American Symphony* was the first composition by an African American composer to be performed by a major symphony orchestra.

Another genre of music that is considered uniquely American is jazz. There are various kinds of jazz, each with distinctive characteristics. Ragtime, blues, instrumental jazz, and concert jazz all have distinguishing traits; but they all have one trait in common: syncopation.

Country music, begun in the early 1920s and Rock and Roll, evolving in the 1950s, have similar rhythms and instrumentation. The lyrics of country music tend to tell a story; rock and roll lyrics cover a wide range of subjects. Both genres were made popular by LP recordings, radio and TV broadcasts, and live performances.

I.   Transition from the Romantic period into the 20th Century

Richard Strauss (1864-1949)

Richard Strauss was born in Munich on June 11, 1864. As early as the age of six, Strauss was already composing his first pieces. By his 18th birthday, he had composed over 140 works. He was a leading German composer of the late Romantic and early modern eras.

Strauss is known for his operas, which include *Der Rosenkavalier, Elektra,* and *Salomé* as well as his tone poems, including *Till Eulenspiegel's Merry Pranks* and *Also sprach Zarathustra.* The operas, *Elektra* and *Salomé,* stretched the limits of dissonance in harmony and in subject matter. He later adjusted his harmonic tendencies to include much less dissonance in the opera *Der Rosenkavalier.* Among his most popular songs are *Cäcilie, Morgen!* and *Traum durch die Dämmerung.*

Tone poem is a one-movement work of program music for orchestra in which the music suggests a story, scene, or mood. The genre of tone poem is also called symphonic poem.

Suggested Search:
Tone Poem
    Till Eulenspiegel's Merry Pranks
    Also sprach Zarathustra
Opera
    Salomé Final Scene (Herodias kisses the head of John the Baptist)
Songs
    Morgen

ANECDOTE:
Once Strauss was asked why he did not leave Germany during the Nazi regime. His response: "Germany had 56 opera houses; the United States had two. It would have reduced my income."

II.   Impressionism

Impressionism is a late 19th-century term for art which avoids clear, precise detail and emphasizes suggestion or impression. A painting by Parisian artist, Claude Monet, entitled *Impression: Sun Rising*, influenced the artistic world and was quickly embraced by other renowned artists.

Suggested Search:
    "Impression: Sun Rising," Claude Monet

Claude Debussy (1862-1918)

Claude Debussy was the leading composer of the movement Impressionism and the most important French composer of his time. Debussy was inspired by the French literary style of his period known as Symbolism. His use of pentatonic and chromatic scales influenced many composers who followed him. His music is known for its tone color and frequent use of non-traditional tonalities.

Suggested Search:
    Clair de lune
    Prelude to the Afternoon of a Faun
    Reverie
    La cathédrale engloutie

III.   Primitivism

Primitivism is a style of art and music that evolved in the early 20th century that was influenced by primitive works of art from pagan cultures. Explorers discovered remote areas around the world and were fascinated with primitive cultures and customs. These new discoveries caused several artists and musicians to become disenchanted with their own "cultured" societies, thereby becoming captivated by "primitive" art. Primitivism led to one of the greatest works of the early 20th century, *The Rite of Spring*.

Igor Stravinsky (1882-1971)

Born near St. Petersburg, Russia, Igor Stravinsky is one of the most influential composers of the 20th century. He was a composer, pianist, and conductor. He first achieved international fame with three ballets: T*he Firebird, Petrushka*, and *The Rite of Spring. The Rite of Spring* transformed the way in which later composers thought about rhythms and was largely responsible for his reputation as a musical revolutionary.

The *Rite of Spring* dealt with fertility rites culminating in the sacrifice of a young maiden to appease the fertility gods. Reaction at the premier of *The Rite of Spring* in Paris, France in 1913 resulted in fist fights among the audience as police were called to restore order.

Suggested Search:
   The Firebird
   Rite of Spring
      "Sacrificial Dance"

IV.   Expressionism

Expressionism is an early 20th-century term in which music looked to convey a disturbed mind; all forms of beauty in music were avoided to express deep personal thoughts. The writings of Sigmund Freud, Viennese psychologist, analyzed dreams to probe secrets of a disturbed mind. He, along with many painters, sculptors and composers of this period, was intrigued by the dark thoughts of the subconscious mind. Edvard Munch's "The Scream" portrayed the terror of society typical of the Expressionist movement.

Suggested Search: "The Scream"

Sprechstimme or Sprechgesang is a vocal style generally associated with the movement Expressionism in which the performer approximates the written pitches on the staff while allowing the voice to "fall away" from the pitch. This technique was largely developed by Arnold Schönberg.

Atonality - An early 20th-century term that avoids showing a central pitch or tonal center in music.

Serialism - Technique of musical composition in the early-mid 20th-century which treats the elements of pitch, rhythm, and dynamics in an organized manner; each element recurs in a continually repeated series.

Twelve-tone technique - A system of atonal music composed of 12 chromatic pitches of the scale arranged in a way that forms the basis for a music composition. This technique ensures that all pitches are sounded before a note can be repeated.

Arnold Schönberg (1874-1951)
   Arnold Schönberg, Austrian composer, music theorist, and painter, was associated with the Expressionist movement in German poetry, art, and music. He created new methods of musical composition involving atonality, using serialism and the twelve-tone technique.

   Suggested Search:
   Pierrot Lunaire, "Moondrunk & Night"
   Peripetie
   Drei Klavierstücke, Op. 11

V.   Experimentalism
   Experimentalism is a trend in early 20th century music which explored new sounds, techniques and other unknown aspects of music. Many composers felt that all possibilities of rhythms, melodies and harmonies had been exhausted; every possible combination had already been composed.

Polytonality - Two or more keys played simultaneously.

Polyrhythm - More than one rhythm used simultaneously.

Tone cluster - A chord built on intervals of a 2nd, usually played by the forearm or fist; strongly associated with Henry Cowell and Charles Ives.

a. Charles Ives (1874-1954)
   Charles Ives is among the most representative of American composers. He is one of the first American composers of international recognition, though his music was largely ignored during his life. He was among the first composers to engage in experimental music, with techniques including polytonality, polyrhythms, tone clusters, and quarter tones.

   Suggested Search:
   Three Places in New England "General Putnam's Camp"
   The Cage
   Shall We Gather at the River

   ANECDOTE:
   Charles Ives studied music at Yale University but chose selling life insurance as a vocation.

   He founded his own insurance company, Ives & Co., in 1907. Later, he joined partner Julian Myrick, and the company was renamed Ives & Myrick; this company became one of the most successful and profitable insurance companies in the United States. Ives and Myrick is now known as Mutual Life.

b. Henry Cowell (1897-1965)

With no formal music education, Henry Cowell became an influential American pianist and composer. He developed what he called the "string piano," a technique in which one strums the piano strings, instead of pressing the keys. He also experimented extensively in aleatory music. His *Mosaic Quartets* allowed performers to take given sheets of music, throw them in the air, then arrange them in any desired order.

Suggested Search:
  Mosaic Quartets
  The Banshee

c. John Cage (1912-1992)

A pioneer of aleatory music and non-standard use of musical instruments, John Cage was one of the leading figures after World War II. He was an American composer, music theorist, writer, philosopher, and artist. Cage is perhaps best known for his 1952 composition *4'33"*, which is performed in the absence of sound; musicians who perform *4'33"* do nothing aside from being present for the duration of four minutes and thirty-three seconds. Cage was fascinated by the importance of silence, not only in music, but in the world around us. He encouraged the audience to listen to the natural sounds around them.

Cage was also a pioneer of the prepared piano, a piano with its sound altered by objects (screws, nuts, bolts, rubber wedges) placed between or on its strings or hammers.

Aleatory music is music in which the elements of composition and/or performance are left to chance, such as tossing coins; a concept that was pioneered by John Cage. One of Cage's most unique compositions is entitled "ASLSP" (As SLow aS Possible) to be performed over a period of 639 years. It is currently being performed on a specially constructed organ in Halberstadt, Germany.

Suggested Search:
4'33"
Prepared Piano
Imaginary Landscape No. 4
Water Walk
As SLow aS Possible

ANECDOTE:

In 1949 John Cage gave a lecture entitled *Lecture on Nothing* at the Artists' Club in New York City. Within his speech was the repetition of the phrase, "If anyone is sleepy let him go to sleep." During the question-and-answer period after the lecture, he gave one of six previously prepared answers regardless of the questions.

d. Pauline Oliveros (1932-2016)

Pauline Oliveros, American composer and prominent figure in the development of experimental music, used tape recordings and other electronic techniques to write music.

Oliveros explored vocal and instrumental tone colors and timbres in unconventional ways. *Sound Patterns* is a choral composition in which the singers use consonants such as sh, s, z, p, t, and others to produce the sounds heard in this piece.

Suggested Search:
Sound Patterns
Part I

VI. American Nationalism

a. Aaron Copland (1900-1990)

Aaron Copland, referred to by his peers and critics as "the Dean of American Composers," was an American composer, music teacher, and conductor. The harmonies in much of his music are typical of what many people consider to be the sound of American music. His compositions evoke the American pioneer spirit. He is best known for the works he wrote in the 1930s and 1940s. Among these are his ballets *Appalachian Spring, Billy the Kid, Rodeo* and the opera, *Tender Land.*

Suggested Search:
Ballets
    Appalachian Spring
        'Tis the Gift to be Simple"
    Billy the Kid.
        "Concert Suite"
    Rodeo
        "Hoe Down"
Opera
    Tender Land
        "The promise of living"
        "Stomp Your Foot"

b. William Grant Still (1895-1978)

William Grant Still, often referred to as "the Dean of African American composers," was an American composer who composed more than 150 works, including five symphonies and eight operas. He was the first African American composer to have an opera produced by the New York City Opera and became the first African American to have a major orchestra play one of his compositions, *Afro-American Symphony.*

Suggested Search:
    Afro-American Symphony, 3rd Movement
    Miniatures for woodwind quintet
        "Ride Ol' Paint," "Frog Went a
        Courtin'," "Jesus is the Rock in a
        Weary Land"

VII.   Opera

George Gershwin (1898-1937)

George Gershwin began his career as a "song plugger," but he soon started composing Broadway theater works with his brother, Ira Gershwin. Gershwin's compositions included both popular and Classic genres, and his most popular melodies are widely known. Among his best-known works are the orchestral compositions *Rhapsody in Blue* and *An American in Paris*, as well as the opera *Porgy and Bess*. *Porgy and Bess*, initially a failure, is now considered one of the most important American operas of the 20th century.

Suggested Search:
    Rhapsody in Blue
    Porgy and Bess
        "Summertime"
        "It Ain't Necessarily So"
        "Oh Lawd, I'm on my way"

VIII.   Musicals

a. Leonard Bernstein (1918-1990)

Leonard Bernstein, American composer, conductor, author, and pianist was one of the first American-born conductors to receive worldwide fame. He was among the first composer/conductors born and educated in the United States to receive worldwide acclaim.

Bernstein's fame was derived from his long tenure as the music director of the New York Philharmonic Orchestra and from his conducting most of the world's leading orchestras. As a composer he wrote in many styles, including symphonies, ballets, film and theater music, choral works, and opera. One of his works for which he is best remembered is the Broadway musical, *West Side Story*.

Suggested Search: West Side Story
"Prologue"
"Cool"
"Tonight"

b. Oscar Hammerstein (1895-1960)
Oscar Hammerstein was an American librettist who collaborated with many composers, such as Jerome Kern and Richard Rodgers to create over 850 songs. Many of his songs are standard repertoire for singers and **jazz** musicians.

c. Jerome Kern (1895-1945)
A native of New York, Jerome Kern created dozens of Broadway musicals and Hollywood films in a career that lasted for more than four decades. He is considered one of the most important American theater composers of the early 20th century. Although many of Kern's musicals were successful, only *Show Boat* is now regularly performed.

Suggested Search: Show Boat "Ol' Man River"
Oscar Hammerstein and Jerome Kern

d. Richard Rodgers (1902-1979)
Some authorities consider Richard Rodgers' contributions to the musical theater of his day extraordinary, and his influence on the musical theater legendary.

Rodgers was an American composer of more than 900 songs and 43 Broadway musicals. He is best known for his partnership with the lyricist Oscar Hammerstein.

Suggested Search:
The Sound of Music
  "The Hills Are Alive"
South Pacific
  "Some Enchanted Evening"
Oklahoma!
  "Oklahoma!"

e. Andrew Lloyd Webber (1948-)

Andrew Lloyd Webber is an English composer of musical theater. Several of his musicals have been successful on Broadway.

He composed 13 musicals, a song cycle, a set of variations, two film scores, and a *Latin Requiem Mass.* Several songs from his musicals have been widely recorded and have become hits such as "The Music of the Night" from *The Phantom of the Opera,* "Don't Cry for Me, Argentina" from *Evita*, and "Memory" from *Cats.*

Suggested Search:
The Phantom of the Opera
  "Music of the Night"
Cats
  "Memory"

IX. Film Music

John Williams (1932-)

John Williams is recognized as one of the most successful and best-known composers of film music today.

Among Williams' greatest successes are *Jaws*, *Indiana Jones,* and *Star Wars.* From 1980 to 1993, Williams conducted the Boston Pops Orchestra. In 1984, he composed the fanfare for the Summer Olympics which has become the official theme song for the Olympic Games. Williams also composed the music used in the openings of the television programs "Meet the Press," "NBC Nightly News," and "The Today Show."

> *Suggested Search:*
> *Jaws*
> > "Jaws Theme"
>
> *Indiana Jones*
> > "Indiana Jones Theme"
>
> *Star Wars*
> > "Main Theme"

X.   Jazz

Jazz is a type of music developed primarily by African Americans in early 20th century characterized by syncopation and improvisation. Some call jazz "America's folk music."

A bill was passed by the U.S. House of Representatives September 23, 1987, and by the Senate December 4, 1987 (H.CON.RES 57), stating the importance of jazz and the preservation of its history. "Now, therefore be it Resolved by the House of Representatives (the Senate concurring), that it is the sense of the Congress that jazz is hereby designated as a rare and valuable national American treasure to which we should devote our attention, support and resources to make certain it is preserved, understood and promulgated."

Jazz was created primarily by African Americans performing in the streets, bars and dance halls of New Orleans.

It is impossible to know exactly how jazz of the early 1900s sounded since most of it existed only in impromptu performances; musical notation was not readily available. Jazz soon evolved into several subtypes: New Orleans jazz (early 1900's), swing (1930's and '40's), and concert jazz (1950's).

XI.   New Orleans Jazz

New Orleans jazz was typically played by a small group of six to eight performers consisting of trumpet, clarinet, and trombone. Occasionally, a cornet was used in place of trumpet. All these players would improvise several melodies simultaneously. The remaining players consisted of drums, double bass, and piano or guitar; occasionally, banjo was used in place of guitar.

    a.   Louis Armstrong (1901-1971)
Louis Armstrong, from New Orleans, LA, was an American trumpeter, bandleader, and singer and was one of the most eminent figures in New Orleans jazz. His career spanned over five decades.

Suggested Search:
Louis Armstrong, "Hotter Than That"
Louis Armstrong, "Trumpet solo"
Louis Armstrong, "When the Saints Go Marchin' In"

ANECDOTE:
Louis Armstrong had a nickname as a child, which referred to the size of his mouth: "Satchel mouth." During a visit to Great Britain, he was met by Percy Brooks, the editor of a well-known British magazine, who greeted him: "Hello, Satchmo!" (A contraction of Satchel mouth).

b. Billie Holliday (1915-1959)
    Billie Holiday was an American jazz singer whose career spanned nearly thirty years. She had a considerable influence on jazz music and pop singing during the 1930s and '50s. She was known for her vocal delivery and improvisational skills which pioneered a new way of singing jazz.

    Suggested Search: Billie Holiday & Louis Armstrong - New Orleans

    Preservation Hall - New Orleans' Preservation Hall was established in 1961 to honor one of America's art forms, New Orleans Jazz. Preservation Hall continues to be popular among jazz enthusiasts today and is a cornerstone of New Orleans music and culture.

    Suggested Search: "Tailgate Ramble" Preservation Hall Jazz Band

XII. Swing and Concert jazz
    Swing is a jazz style that appeared in the 1930s and '40s played mainly by "Big bands," characterized by a danceable, bouncy, swing style. Concert jazz is a style of jazz that appeared in the 1950s that is more relaxed and that uses written arrangements.

    a. Duke Ellington (1899-1974)
        One of the originators of big-band jazz, Duke Ellington was an American composer, pianist and bandleader who composed several jazz concert works over his 50-year career. He is recognized today as one of America's most outstanding musicians.

        Suggested Search:
            Duke Ellington - Mood Indigo
            Duke Ellington, "Take the A Train"

b. Glenn Miller (1904-1944)

Glenn Miller, trombonist and American big band musician, arranger, composer, and bandleader was one of the best-selling recording artists during the swing era (Big Band era) in the 1930s and '40s. Some of his most popular recordings include "In the Mood," "Pennsylvania 6-5000," and "Moonlight Serenade." While he was traveling to entertain U.S. troops in France during World War II, Miller's aircraft disappeared in severe weather over the English Channel.

Suggested Search:
Glenn Miller – "In the Mood" (1941) 4K
"Pennsylvania 6-5000" Live remote from Hotel Pennsylvania.
"Moonlight Serenade"

c. Benny Goodman (1909-1986)

Benny Goodman, known as "The King of Swing," during the Big Band era in the 1930s and '40s, achieved multiple hit songs as a band leader before World War II. As a clarinet virtuoso and conductor, his band was the first jazz band to play Carnegie Hall in the late 1930s.

Suggested Search:
Benny Goodman "Sing Sing Sing 1938
Carnegie Hall
"St. Louis Blues"
Benny Goodman Quartet - Moonglow

d. Tommy Dorsey (1905-1956)

Tommy Dorsey was an American trombonist, composer, conductor and bandleader of the Big Band era (swing era). He is best remembered for his songs such as "Sentimental Over You" and his greatest hit single, "I'll Never Smile Again." This hit song featured a young vocalist, Frank Sinatra.

Suggested Search:
Tommy Dorsey Plays I'm Getting Sentimental Over You
"Las Vegas Nights" 1941. "I'll Never Smile Again" (Frank Sinatra)
The above excerpt is from the movie "Las Vegas Nights" 1941.

XIII.   Ragtime

Ragtime is a style of piano music flourished during the 1890s and early 1900s and was performed principally by black Americans in night clubs and dance halls, primarily in cities such as New Orleans, LA and St. Louis, MO. Its style consisted of the right hand playing a syncopated melody while the left hand kept a steady, march-like bass; associated with Scott Joplin.

a.   Scott Joplin (1868-1917)

Scott Joplin, an American composer and pianist achieved fame for his ragtime compositions and was called the "King of Ragtime." In addition to his ragtime piano pieces, he wrote one ragtime ballet and two operas. One of his most popular works, the "Maple Leaf Rag," has been recognized as the earliest rag. "The Entertainer" is another classic of ragtime which received international prominence in the 1970s, when it was used as the theme music for the film "The Sting," starring Paul Newman and Robert Redford.

Suggested Search:
"Maple Leaf Rag"
"The Entertainer" (Original recording)

b. Jelly Roll Morton (1890-1941)
    Ferdinand J. La Menthe, known professionally as
    Jelly Roll Morton, was an American ragtime and
    early jazz pianist who began his career in New
    Orleans, LA. He later became a composer who began
    the use of prearranged, rehearsed music in jazz
    performances.

    Suggested Search:
        "Tiger Rag" 1938
        "Finger Breaker" - Jelly Roll Morton Piano
        Roll 1938

XIV. Blues
    Blues is a term that refers to a vocal style that appeared
from the African American spiritual or folk song that became
associated with jazz; characterized by flatted or "blue" notes
in the scale (See blue note in the Glossary).

    a. Mamie Smith (1891-1946)
        Mamie Smith, an American singer, dancer, and
        pianist, performed in several styles as a Vaudeville
        singer, including jazz and blues. In 1920, she became
        the first African American artist to make vocal blues
        recordings.

        Suggested Search: Mamie Smith "Crazy Blues"
        1920

    b. Bessie Smith (1894-1937)
        Nicknamed the "Empress of the Blues," Bessie
        Smith was the most popular female blues singer of
        the 1920s and 1930s. She is often regarded as one of
        the greatest singers of her era and was a major
        influence on later jazz singers.

        Suggested Search:
            Bessie Smith "Careless Love Blues" 1925

Bessie Smith "Lost Your Head Blues" 1926

c. Rosetta Tharpe (1915-1973)

Rosetta Tharpe was a gospel, jazz, and blues singer born in Cotton Plant, AR. She became popular in the 1930s and ′40s with her gospel recordings, which included both spiritual texts and rhythmic accompaniment that, according to some of her contemporary musicians, was a forerunner of rock and roll. Tharpe brought spiritual music into the mainstream by gospel music in nightclubs and concert halls accompanied by big bands.

Suggested Search:
Sister Rosetta Tharpe - Up Above My Head on Gospel Time TV show
Sister Rosetta Tharp "Didn't It Rain" Live in Manchester England.

The above excerpt is from a live performance of Rosetta Tharpe with 'Didn't It Rain' 1964 in Manchester, England as part of The British Tours of "The American Folk Blues Festival."

d. B. B. King (1925-2015)

Riley B. King, better known as B. B. King, was an American blues singer, electric guitarist, and songwriter. He introduced a style of solo guitar based on string bending vibrato that influenced many later electric blues guitarists. King was born on a cotton plantation in Itta Bena, MS. At an early age, he was attracted to music and the guitar in church and began his career in nightclubs and local radio. He later lived in Memphis, Tennessee, and Chicago. His career spanned 1949 to 2014. King died at the age of 89 in Las Vegas, Nevada, on May 14, 2015.

Suggested Search:
B.B. King "The Thrill Is Gone" (Live at Montreux 1993)

Suggested Search:

B. B. King "Best Performance Ever"

The above excerpt is from a performance at Sing Sing Prison in New York City in 1972.

ANECDOTE:

In the winter of 1949, King played at a dance hall in Twist, AR. The hall was heated by a kerosene heater set in the middle of the dance floor. During the evening, two men began to fight, knocking over the barrel and causing the dance floor to be engulfed in flames.

The hall was at once evacuated. Once outside, King realized that he had left his guitar inside, so he went back into the burning building to save his beloved guitar. King learned that the two men that started the fire had been fighting over a woman named Lucille, who worked as a hostess at the dance hall. King named his guitar "Lucille" as a reminder never again to do something as foolish as run into a burning building or fight over a woman.

XV.   Country Music and Its Subcultures

Country music can be traced back to Appalachian folk music around the turn of the 20th century, particularly in eastern Tennessee; it was originally referred to as "hillbilly music." Most historians agree that the recordings of Jimmie Rodgers and the Carter Family in the 1920s marked the beginning of country music. Jimmie Rodgers, known as the "Father of Country Music," recorded the first single recording to sell one million copies, "Blue Yodel #1." The Carter family is recognized as the first vocal group to become famous, with their popular recording, "Wildwood Flower."

Jimmie Rodgers (1897-1933) was an American singer-songwriter from Meridian, MS who was popular in the late 1920s.

He is best known for his distinctive style of yodeling. He recorded over 100 songs during a six-year period. He was diagnosed with tuberculosis when he was a young man and died at the age of 37.

Suggested Search: Jimmie Rodgers "Blue Yodel #1"

The Carter Family was a singing group that recorded American folk music of the Appalachian Mountains between 1927 and mid-1950s. They recorded over 300 songs, many of which were ballads, humorous songs, and religious songs. Member of the original group were A. P. Carter, his wife, Sara, and A. P.'s sister, Maybelle. Later the group included three daughters of Maybelle, Anita, Helen, and June, who married Johnny Cash.

Suggested Search: The Carter Family "Wildwood Flower"

Bluegrass music is considered a branch of country music, and while similar, there are differences. Bluegrass usually consists of two or three-part harmony with a distinctive high voice; country music usually features a solo singer. Bluegrass uses a banjo and mandolin, while country utilizes more guitar and fiddle instrumentation.

Bill Monroe (1911-1996), the "Father of Bluegrass" first popularized bluegrass which was named after his band, "Bill Monroe and the Blue Grass Boys." Monroe's home state was Kentucky, known as the "Bluegrass State."

Suggested Search: Bill Monroe and the Blue Grass Boys "Uncle Pen

In the early 1940s, a new brand of country music referred to as "Honky-tonk" received national attention. Instrumentation included guitars and added a steel guitar. This style was represented by artists such as Ernest Tubb and Hank Williams.

Ernest Tubb (1914-1984) was born on a cotton farm in Crisp, Texas, just south of Dallas. His father was a sharecropper and Tubb spent his formative years working on farms throughout Texas. He was inspired by Jimmie Rodger and spent his spare time learning to play the guitar and yodel. His single recording "Walking the Floor Over You" sold over one million copies and brought Tubb to stardom.

Suggested Search: Ernest Tubb "Walkin' the Floor Over You"

Hank Williams (1923-1953), born in Georgiana, Alabama, is considered by many to be America's first country music superstar. He began playing guitar at age eight and made his first appearance on radio at age 13; the next year he formed his own band. He alternated from Mobile to Montgomery while he toured throughout the southern United States. He died at the age of 29 after a life of alcohol abuse in attempts to ease his back pain.

Suggested Search:
  Hank Williams "I'm So Lonesome, I Could Cry" 1949
  Hank Williams "Hey, Good Lookin'" 1951
  Hank Williams "Your Cheatin' Heart" 1952

The Nashville Sound brought a fresh style of country music in the mid-1950s which sounded sophisticated and polished. This new sound replaced the "Honky Tonk" sound popular during the 1940s and early 1950s. Artists such as Chet Atkins, Eddy Arnold, Patsy Cline, and Jim Reeves helped to create this new mellow, lyrical style.

Chet Atkins (1924 – 2001), sometimes called "Mr. Guitar," was an American musician who helped create the Nashville Sound.

Atkins' particular guitar picking style (picking with his first three fingers, with the thumb on bass) and musicianship brought him popularity both in the United States and abroad. He was an executive for RCA Victor Records from 1958 until 1974, producing recordings for such artists as Elvis Presley, Eddy Arnold and Jim Reeves.

Suggested Search: "10 of Chet Atkins' Most Memorable Songs"

Eddy Arnold (1918-2008) was an American country music singer who performed for over sixty years. Early in his career, he became a member of the Grand Old Opry. He was one of the first country music artists to work as a television performer. He hosted his own shows, *Eddy Arnold Time* in 1955 and *The Eddy Arnold Show* in 1956.

Suggested Search:
Eddy Arnold – "Cattle Call" 1944
Eddy Arnold – "You Don't Know Me" 1960
Eddy Arnold – "Make the World Go Away 1965

Patsy Cline (1932-1963) was born in Camden, Tennessee, but spent most of her adult life in Nashville; she became one of the top singers of the "Nashville Sound." She preferred country ballads, especially melancholy love songs, which she recorded and performed on television in the 1950s-60s. In March 1963, she was killed in a plane crash at the age of 30, along with her manager.

Suggested Search:
Patsy Cline "Walkin' After Midnight" 1957
Patsy Cline "Crazy" 1961
Patsy Cline "I Fall to Pieces" 1961

Jim Reeves (1923-1964), known as "Gentleman Jim," was a well-known contributor to the "Nashville Sound." He was born in a rural community near Carthage, Texas. He received an athletic scholarship to the University of Texas but soon dropped out to play professional baseball with the St. Louis Cardinals in 1944. He played for three years before an injury ended his athletic career.

Suggested Search:
    Jim Reeves "Four Walls" 1957
    Jim Reeves "He'll Have to Go" 1960

Outlaw Country, a subgenre of country music, describes a movement that began in the 1970s as a reaction to the Nashville Sound, which many felt had become too commercialized. This style blended a bit of honky-tonk and rock and roll. Willie Nelson, Merle Haggard, and Waylon Jennings were among the popular singers, while "the man in black," Johnny Cash was the most famous.

Willie Nelson (1933-) was a pioneer of the movement that led to the genre Outlaw Country. His album *Shotgun Willie* was released in June 1973 and was one of the first albums of Outlaw Country.

Suggested Search:
    Willie Nelson - Shotgun Willie (Live from Austin
    City Limits)
    Willie Nelson "On the Road Again"

Merle Haggard (1937-2016) was born in Oildale, California during the years of The Great Depression. The death of his father left his family destitute. His childhood was troubled and he was incarcerated several times in his youth. After being released from San Quentin State Prison in 1960, he was able to begin a successful country music career.

Suggested Search:
    Merle Haggard "Mama Tried"
    Merle Haggard "Okie from Muskogee"

Waylon Arnold Jennings (1937 – 2002) started playing guitar at the age of eight and performed at age fourteen on local radio stations, after which he formed his first band. He left high school at age 16 and worked as a performer and disc jockey on several radio stations around Phoenix, Arizona. In 1958, Buddy Holly hired him to play bass in his band, "The Crickets." At the time, Holly and his band were playing tours across the Midwest. Rather than travel by bus, Holly chose to charter a plane to reach their next performance in Moorehead, Minnesota. Another band member was sick and Jennings gave up his seat on the plane and rode the bus; the plane crashed, killing all four on board.

Jennings composed and sang the theme song for the TV show *The Dukes of Hazzard* and provided narration for the show.

Suggested Search:
Waylon Jennings "Dukes of Hazzard Theme"
Waylon Jennings "Good Hearted Woman"

Johnny Cash (1932-2003), known as "The Man in Black," was born in Kingsland, Arkansas, to a family of sharecroppers. In his childhood, he was exposed to hymns, gospel songs, and ballads sung while working in the fields with his family. After a term in the military in the mid-1950s, he moved to Memphis, Tennessee where he pursued a career in music.

Two songs, "Folsom Prison Blues" and "I Walk the Line" recorded on Sun Records in 1955 gained him recognition on the country music scene. His television show, *The Johnny Cash Show* in 1969 introduced Cash to a larger audience and opened the door to such venues as Carnegie Hall and the White House.

In 1968, Johnny Cash and June Carter, daughter of Maybelle Carter of the "Carter Family," were married. She was a regular performer on *The Johnny Cash Show.*

Suggested Search:
Johnny Cash: "Folsom Prison Blues – Live at San Quentin"

Johnny Cash "I Walk the Line"
Johnny Cash, June Carter Cash - Jackson (The Best of
The Johnny Cash TV Show)

XVI.   Rock and Roll
In the mid-1950s, the term "Rock and Roll" was evolving
from a union of two styles of singing: rhythm and blues and
country music. In 1955, Bill Haley and the Comets recorded
"Rock Around the Clock," which appealed to a wide
audience, primarily made up of young people. This new style
of singing was made popular by singers like Buddy Holly,
Elvis Presley, Little Richard, Jerry Lee Lewis, Fats Domino,
and Chuck Berry.
Bill Haley (1925-1981) became a superstar in the 1950s
after releasing "Shake, Rattle and Roll" and "Rock Around
the Clock." "Rock Around the Clock" was featured in the
1955 film *Blackboard Jungle,* a movie about high school
students rebelling against teachers and authority. It would be
featured again in the 1970s as the theme for the television
series *Happy Days.*

Suggested Search:
Bill Haley and the Comets "Shake, Rattle, and Roll"
Bill Haley and the Comets "Rock Around the Clock,"
1954.

Buddy Holley (1936 – 1959) was an American singer who
was prominent in the development of rock and roll in the
mid-1950s. He made his first appearance on local television
in 1952 with his group performing country music but after
opening for Bill Haley and His Comets that year, his band's
style shifted from country music to rock and roll; he named
his group "The Crickets." In September 1957, "That'll Be the
Day" and "Peggy Sue" were major hits.
In 1959, a private plane carrying Buddy Holly and other
musicians crashed outside of Clear Lake, Iowa, killing all on
board. Buddy Holly had chartered the flight to avoid riding
the bus; Waylon Jennings, band member, gave up his seat on
the plane. Holly was 22.

Suggested Search:
 Buddy Holly "That'll Be the Day"
 Buddy Holly & The Crickets "Peggy Sue" on The Ed
 Sullivan Show

Elvis Presley (1935-1977), a dominant performer of rock and roll during the mid-1950s until his death, was widely known as "The King of Rock and Roll." His music was a blend of country, gospel, and rhythm and blues. His musical influence came from songs he heard on the radio, his parents' Pentecostal church, and from night clubs on Beale Street in Memphis.

His first hit song, "That's alright, Mama," was recorded in 1954 and set the style of his next recordings over the next year. By1955, Presley had developed a following with fans being attracted to his new musical style and provocative movements. That same year, he signed with RCA Records, recording his first No. One single with "Heartbreak Hotel." He also signed a movie contract with Paramount Pictures to star in the movie *Love Me Tender* in 1956. That same year, he had a series of hits: "Don't Be Cruel" and "Love Me Tender;" "All Shook Up" followed in 1957. He also became a popular guest on a number of television variety shows.

After a stint in the Army in 1960, Presley resumed his career and continued recording music and acting in such films as *Gi Blues* (1960)*, Blue Hawaii* (1961), *Girls! Girls! Girls!* (1962) and *Viva Las Vegas* (1964). He continued to perform in Las Vegas where he remained a popular attraction and also toured throughout the United States. He performed at his last concert in June 1977. On the morning of August 16, 1977, Elvis Presley died of heart failure. He was 42.

Suggested Search:
 Elvis Presley "That's Alright, Mama" 1954
 Elvis Presley "Hound Dog," 1956.
 Elvis Presley "Jailhouse Rock" (1957) Classic Movie
 Musical Numbers
 Elvis Presley "American Trilogy"

Richard Wayne Penniman (1932-2020), known as "Little Richard," was an American singer and pianist who significantly influenced the development of rock and roll in the mid-1950s. His first big hit, "Tutti Frutti," was recorded in New Orleans in 1955. His later hits, "Good Golly, Miss Molly" and "Long Tall Sally" with screams, wails, along with non-sensical lyrics, attracted an audience of primarily of teenagers. His later performances were embellished with gyrations, excessive eyeliner and overdone makeup.

Suggested Search:
   Little Richards "Tutti Frutti" 1955
   Little Richards "Long Tall Sally" 1956

Jerry Lee Lewis (1935-2022) was a pioneer of early rock and roll and sometimes described as rock and roll's first "wild man." His first big hit "Whole Lot a Shakin' Going On" brought him worldwide attention. His popularity dropped drastically when he married his 13-year old cousin in 1957 which almost ended his career. In 1968, he crossed over to country music with a another hit, "Another Place, Another Time." Throughout the 1960s and 70s, Lewis had over 30 popular hits.

Suggested Search:
   Jerry Lee Lewis – "Whole Lotta Shakin' Goin' On" (Steve Allen Show 1957)
   Jerry Lee Lewis – "Another Place, Another Time"

Antoine Domino, Jr. "Fats Domino" (1928-2017) was an American singer and pianist from New Orleans and one of the first artists to help define rock and roll. His recordings "Ain't That a Shame" (1955) and "Blueberry Hill" (1956) brought him widespread fame. He died of natural causes in his hometown of New Orleans on October 24, 2017.

Suggested Search:
   Fats Domino "Ain't That a Shame" 1956.

Fats Domino "Blueberry Hill" on Ed Sullivan Show 1956.

Chuck Berry (1926-2017) was an American rhythm and blues singer, songwriter, and guitarist who played a significant role in the evolution of rock and roll. He blended elements of rhythm and blues and early rock in songs such as "Mabellene" and "Johnny B. Goode." He was known for his showmanship and virtuosity on the guitar.

Suggested Search:
Chuck Berry "Back in the USA" 1959.
Chuck Berry, "Johnny B. Goode" 1958.

In 1964, a rock and roll group from Liverpool, England, The Beatles, made their US debut on the popular television program *The Ed Sullivan Show*. The reception of the Beatles by American audiences opened the door for other British groups, such as The Rolling Stones, to come to America.

The Beatles, comprised of John Lennon, Paul McCartney, George Harrison, and Ringo Starr, incorporated various styles of music creating their own unique sound. They were especially popular among the youth of the 1960s and were influential in the counterculture of the 1960s.

Suggested Search:
Beatles, "Twist and Shout" 1964
The Beatles – "A Hard Day's Night" 1964
The Beatles – "I Want To Hold Your Hand" The Ed Sullivan Show 1964

The Rolling Stones, a rock band formed in London in 1962 and featuring Mick Jagger, generated a negative image and by the 1980s, new styles would appear: heavy metal and hard rock. They were active for over 60 years and became identified with the rebellious youth culture of the 1960s.

Suggested Search: Rolling Stones "Satisfaction" 1965

These new sounds of rock and roll, heavy meal, and hard rock, along with bizarre, sometimes shocking, behavior appealed to youth audiences across America. Concerts were enhanced by elaborate lighting and sound effects.

This brief discussion of rock and roll has named only a small group of individuals significant to the development of this genre. Rock and roll is undoubtedly here to stay as predicted by a group called Danny and the Juniors:

> "Rock 'n roll is here to stay; it will never die. It was meant to be that way, though I don't know why. I don't care what people say, rock 'n roll is here to stay."
>
> *Suggested Search: Rockin' with Danny and the Juniors*, released 1958.

Glossary

Absolute music Instrumental music that contains no association with a program, story, or poem of any kind. Example: *Symphony No. 5 in C Minor*.

A cappella (Italian) "In chapel style." Group singing without instrumental accompaniment.

Accelerando (Italian) To gradually get faster; increase the pace.

Accent Emphasis or stress placed on a musical beat.

Aleatory (See Chance music) Music in which the elements of composition and/or performance are left to chance, such as tossing coins; a concept that was pioneered by John Cage.

Alto, contralto A low female voice or high male voice.

Antiphonal A term which describes a performance in which two or more groups alternate singing or playing instruments.

Aria (Italian) Vocal solo in an opera, oratorio, or cantata with orchestral accompaniment. In an aria, the words, "I seek revenge" might be sung several times to fully express the emotion of the moment. Unlike the recitative, the aria, with a beautiful melody, could last for several minutes.

Art song (See *Lied*) A song in which the piano accompaniment, poetic text and melody are of equal importance, usually through composed and requiring high standards of performance.

Atonal, atonality (See Tonic) An early 20th-century term that avoids establishing a central pitch or tonal center in music.

Ballad opera Genre of 18th-century comic plays popular in England and Ireland featuring songs in English. The texts were usually satirical poking fun at English political or social life and Italian opera, very popular in London at that time.

Ballet A form of classical dance that originated in France during the Baroque period.

Band A large instrumental ensemble consisting of brass, woodwind, and percussion instruments; this group is sometimes called a symphonic band.

Bar (See Measure) A rhythmic group of notes and rests located between bar lines on a staff.

Baritone A medium-range male voice.

Baroque Term originally meaning "miss-shaped pearl;" period of music history from approximately 1600 to 1750.

Bass A low male voice.

Bass drum A percussion instrument of indefinite pitch played with a large soft mallet; the largest drum in band or orchestra.

Bassoon A double-reed woodwind instrument with a low range; it is the principal woodwind bass instrument in an orchestra. The sound is made by blowing air into a mouthpiece which then causes the two reeds to vibrate.

Basso continuo (Italian) A system of musical "shorthand" used in the Baroque period in which a melody and an instrumental bass line are written on a staff. Another instrument, such as keyboard or lute, then fills in the harmony by playing the figured bass, i.e., numbers, sharps or flats written beneath the staff.

Bayreuth Theater An opera house in Bayreuth, Germany, designed and constructed by Richard Wagner for the exclusive performances of his operas, which he called "music dramas."

Beat A recurring rhythmic pulse of music.

Bel canto (Italian) "Beautiful singing." Elegant Italian vocal style of the early 19th century that emphasized the beauty, agility, and virtuosity of the human voice; typically associated with the castrato.

Big band A style of music popular between World War I and World War II performed by a large jazz ensemble; sometimes referred to as "swing,"

Blue note In jazz and blues, a blue note is a note that is sung or played at a slightly different pitch than standard, typically between a quartertone and a semitone.

Blues A term referring to a vocal style that emerged from the African American spiritual or folk song that became associated with jazz; characterized by flatted or "blue" notes in the Scale.

Brass family A family of instruments made of brass or silver whose sound is produced by buzzing the lips into a mouthpiece; the pitch is varied by valves or slides.

Cadence The close of musical phrase.

Cantata (Italian "sung") In the 17th and 18th centuries, a vocal chamber work on a religious or secular subject that includes several movements with recitatives and arias; shorter than an oratorio.

Castrato (Italian) Male singer castrated before puberty to preserve the high vocal range, prominent during the 17th and 18th centuries, especially in opera and oratorio.

Cello A bowed string instrument with a range lower than a viola and higher than a double bass. Originally called violoncello.

Chamber Music Music for a small group that is performed in a home or small auditorium, with one player to a part.

Chance music (See Aleatory)

Chimes A percussion instrument of definite pitch which consists of suspended metal tubes of various lengths that are struck with hammers.

Chorale A type of hymn sung by the congregation in the Lutheran Church; introduced by Martin Luther.

Chord A harmony consisting of three or more notes heard simultaneously.

Chromatic scale A scale that utilizes all twelve pitches, equally divided, within the octave.

Clarinet A single-reed woodwind instrument. The sound is made by blowing air into a mouthpiece which then causes the reed to vibrate.

Classic period In music history, the era from approximately 1750 to 1825. The music of the Classic period was dominated primarily by two composers: Franz Joseph Haydn and Wolfgang Amadeus Mozart. During this period most of the significant developments in music occurred in instrumental forms: the symphony, concerto, sonata, and in chamber Music.

Clavichord A small keyboard instrument that produces a soft sound, developed during the Renaissance and used mostly in private homes. The tone is created by a small metal tangent that strikes the strings.

Clavier A generic term for any musical instrument having a keyboard such as a harpsichord, clavichord, or piano.

Coda An optional concluding section of a symphony following the recapitulation section of sonata-allegro form.

Col legno (Italian) Indication that a performer is to play a violin, viola, cello, or double bass with the wooden part of the bow.

Comic opera A sung dramatic work of a light or comic nature, usually with spoken dialogue and written in the vernacular.

Concert jazz A style of jazz that emerged in the 1950s that is more relaxed and that utilizes written arrangements in place of improvisation.

Concerto A multi-movement work for the orchestra and an instrumental soloist.

Concerto grosso A multi-movement instrumental work that uses a small ensemble of solo instruments along with a larger group of instruments.

Concertmaster A member of the orchestra, usually the principal violinist, who is the assistant to the conductor.

Conductor A person who leads performances of music ensembles such as bands, orchestras, or choirs; also known as a director.

Consonance Interval or chord that has a pleasing, stable sound.

Cornet A brass instrument similar to the trumpet but with a more mellow tone.

Council of Trent Prompted by the Protestant Reformation, the Council of Trent was primarily responsible for self-reform within the Roman Catholic Church. It played a vital role in revitalizing the Roman Catholic Church in many parts of Europe.

Counterpoint (See Polyphony) Combination of two or more melodic lines.

Counter Reformation Name for the period the Roman Catholic Church initiated in response to the Protestant Reformation; it began with the Council of Trent.

Crescendo (Italian) A gradual increase in the volume of sound.

Cymbals Percussion instruments of indefinite pitch consisting of two large plates that are struck together.

Development (See Sonata-allegro form) In sonata-allegro form, the second section, after the Exposition, presents the themes in various keys.

Diatonic scale (See Major scale) A scale that consists of five whole steps and two half steps to form the familiar scale of Western music. The result is a seven-note pattern of tones that ascends in the following order of whole steps and half steps: 1 - 1 - ½ - 1 - 1 - 1 - ½.

*Diminuendo, Decrescendo (*Italian) A gradual decrease in the volume of sound.

Dissonance Two or more tones sounding together to produce "unsettled" sounds, giving a feeling of unrest.

Double bass The largest member of the bowed string family, having the lowest range.

Dynamics, Dynamic level Loudness or softness of a tone.

English horn A double-reed woodwind instrument in the oboe family. It is approximately one and a half times the length of an oboe and sounds lower in range. The sound is made by blowing air into a mouthpiece which then causes the two reeds to vibrate.

Emfindsam Stil (German) "sensitive style" An emotional style of music closely associated with the Rococo style as practiced by the German middle class of the late 18th century, with less emphasis on elegance and featuring sudden harmonic changes.

Enlightenment The Enlightenment was an intellectual and philosophical movement which dominated Europe during the 18th century. This period was characterized by revolutions in religion, science, philosophy, society and politics.

Ensemble finale The final scene of an opera or musical in which the principal singers return to the stage and simultaneously perform different words and music.

Equal temperament Another term for equal tuning. A system of tuning in which the octave is divided into 12 equal half-steps (semitones); the most common system of tuning used in Western music.

Experimentalism, Experimental music A trend in early 20th-century music that explored new sounds, techniques and other unknown aspects of music.

Exposition (See Sonata-allegro form) In sonata-allegro form, the first section in which the main themes are introduced.

Expressionism Early 20th-century term in which music sought to convey a disturbed mind; all forms of beauty in music were avoided in order to express deep personal thoughts.

Figured bass (See Basso continuo) Numbers, flats or sharps that are placed beneath the bass line to indicate the harmony to be played.

Flute A woodwind instrument, made of metal, with a high range; held horizontally, its tone is produced by blowing across a hole.

Form The overall design and organization of a composer's work.

Forte (Italian) In musical notation, a dynamic marking meaning "loud;" often abbreviated *f.*

Fortissimo (Italian) In musical notation, a dynamic marking meaning "very loud;" often abbreviated *ff.*

Florentine Camerata A group of intellectuals in Florence, Italy who met regularly during mid-1500's and who believed that polyphony was inadequate to express drama effectively. They argued that only a single melodic line, sung by a solo voice (monody), could adequately portray the meaning of poetry.

French horn A brass instrument of a medium range whose tubing is coiled into a circle. It is played by depressing valves. Sometimes referred to as horn.

Fugue (See Round) A polyphonic composition based on a theme (subject) with successive statements of the theme at different pitches.

Gesamtkunstwerk (German) "Union of the Arts." term used by Richard Wagner in his music dramas in which music, acting, dance, staging, and scenic designs are all merged into one production.

Ground bass (See Ostinato) A repeated melodic pattern in the bass while a melody above it changes.

Harmony Simultaneous combination of tones which form chords.

Harp A plucked string instrument with the strings stretched over a frame in the shape of a triangle.

Harpsichord A popular keyboard instrument of the Baroque and Classic periods; its strings were plucked by a small plectrum or quill.

Heiligenstadt Testament A letter written by Beethoven to his brothers to come to terms with his deafness; considered to be like a last will and testament.

Hob. Abbreviation for Anthony Hoboken, who compiled a catalogue of the musical compositions by Joseph Haydn. Works by Haydn are often indicated using their Hoboken catalogue number, rather than opus.

Homophony, homophonic Musical texture in which a melody is accompanied by chords producing harmony; a hymn is an example of this texture.

Humanism A movement during the Renaissance that stressed the potential value and goodness of human beings along with a renewed interest in ancient art and cultures. This movement originated in northern Italy during the 13th and 14th centuries and later spread through continental Europe and England. Emphasis was placed on the value of human beings, individually and collectively, and focused on critical thinking and evidence over acceptance of tradition or superstition.

Idiomatic writing Music that is written for a specific instrument, considering the instrument's special capabilities, i.e., range, timbre.

Impressionism Late 19th-century term for art and music that avoids clear, precise detail and emphasizes suggestion or impression.

Intermezzo (Italian) Genre of Italian comic opera performed between the acts of a serious opera; forerunner of opera buffa.

Interval Distance between two tones.

Jazz A type of music developed primarily by African Americans in the early 20th century, characterized by syncopation and improvisation.

K. Abbreviation for Ludwig von Köchel, who compiled a catalog of W.A. Mozart's works.

Leitmotif (German) A device in which a recurring melodic or harmonic fragment is associated with a person, event, mood, or object; used primarily by Richard Wagner in his music dramas.

Libretto (Italian) Text of an opera, oratorio, or other dramatic work.

Lied, (Singular) *lieder* (Plural) (See Art song; German) A song in which the piano accompaniment, poetic text and melody are of equal importance, usually through composed and requiring high standards of performance.

Liturgy The prescribed order of texts that are spoken or sung in a religious service.

Lute A plucked string instrument most widely used during the Middle Ages, Renaissance, and Baroque periods; typically has a pear-shaped body with a rounded back.

Madrigal A polyphonic secular song begun in Italy during the 14th century which also became popular in England; sung in the vernacular.

Major scale (See Diatonic scale) A scale that consists of five whole steps and two half steps to form the familiar scale of Western music. The result is a seven-note pattern of tones that ascends in the following order of whole steps and half steps: 1 - 1 - ½ - 1 - 1 - 1 - ½.

Mass The primary service of the Roman Catholic Church; a musical setting of the Ordinary of the Mass, i.e., *Kyrie, Gloria, Credo, Sanctus*, and *Agnus Dei*.

Measure (See Bar) A rhythmic group of notes and rests located between bar lines on a staff.

Melody A succession of tones perceived as a meaningful line.

Meter A term that denotes the organization of rhythm into regular patterns of strong and weak beats; often referred to as "time signature;" numbers such as $^3_4$ indicate the meter.

Metrical psalm A psalm set to meter, rhythm, and melody.

Minor scale An ascending pattern of seven tones in the following order of whole steps and half steps: 1 - ½ - 1 - 1 - ½ - 1 – 1.

Minuet and Trio A form based on two dances which consists of three parts, A B A (minuet, trio, minuet); usually, the 3rd movement of a symphony or sonata.

Monody A solo song accompanied by one or more instruments.

Monophony, monophonic A single unaccompanied melodic line; can be sung by multiple Voices.

Motet A polyphonic vocal form. The exact meaning of motet changes during music history. After the 15th century, any polyphonic setting of a sacred text in Latin (not Mass) could be called a motet.

Movement A section of a complete work with its own form but conceived as part of a whole composition, such as a symphony with four movements.

Music drama Genre of music created by Richard Wagner in the 19th century in which the music and drama are of equal importance.

Musical A stage or film production which utilizes popular-style songs along with dialogue to tell a story.

Nationalism A Romantic era movement in which artists and composers turned from the prevailing Germanic influence on the arts to include folk songs, dances and legends from their own homelands.

Oboe A double-reed woodwind instrument with a medium-high range. The sound is made by blowing air into a mouthpiece which then causes the two reeds to vibrate.

Octave An interval comprising the first and eighth notes of a major or minor scale; an interval of an eighth, as from C to C.

Opera A dramatic vocal form with continuous, or nearly continuous, singing along with scenery, costumes, and acting.

Opera buffa (Italian) Italian comic opera of the 18th century.

Opéra comique (French) In the 18th century, a light French comic opera, which used spoken dialogue; in the 19th century, could be either comic or tragic.

Opera seria (Italian, "serious opera") Italian opera of the 18th century based on a serious subject, usually a mythological theme.

Operetta Sometimes called light opera, it is a comic form of musical theater. It includes spoken dialogue often with patter songs.

Opus (Latin, "work") A chronological order of works or collection of works by a composer.

Oratorio Genre of dramatic vocal music based on a religious theme, usually taken from the Old Testament, that originated in the 17th century; performed in concert style, it was like an unstaged opera with no acting, costumes nor scenery.

Oratory "Prayer chapel"; oratorios were first performed in prayer chapels (oratories) rather than in concert halls or private homes. Hence, the name oratorio.

Orchestra An ensemble of strings, woodwinds, brass, and percussion instruments, with more than one player on a part.

Pants role (See Trousers role) A male role, usually for an adolescent, performed by a female Singer.

Passion A musical setting of the arrest, trial, and crucifixion of Jesus based on the accounts taken from the New Testament; similar to oratorio and cantata in style.

Patronage system During the Classic period, many musicians worked under what is known as the patronage system. Musicians and/or composers would work as servants to powerful and wealthy noblemen, writing and performing pieces for their patron.

Patter song A setting of humorous words sung very rapidly; typically found in operetta.

Pentatonic scale A five-note scale often found in folk music and non-Western music.

Percussion family A family of instruments of either definite or indefinite pitch whose sound is made by striking with hammer/stick, by shaking or by scraping.

Pianissimo In musical notation, a dynamic marking meaning "very soft;" often abbreviated *pp*.

Piano (Italian) In musical notation, a dynamic marking meaning "soft;" often abbreviated *p;* also refers to a keyboard instrument.

Piano An acoustic, stringed musical instrument invented in Italy by Bartolomeo Cristofori around the year 1700, in which the strings are struck by hammers; pedals control dampers (felt-covered pads) on the strings that stop the sound when the keys are released. Considered part of the percussion family because of its location within the orchestra; see *Pianoforte*.

Pianoforte (Italian, "soft-loud") Early name for a keyboard instrument invented in early 1700's that uses a mechanism to strike the strings and so named because of the ability to vary the tone from "soft to loud" by using pedals and dampers; this is one of the main differences from the harpsichord. Occasionally, but rarely, referred to as *fortepiano*. This instrument is commonly referred to today as a piano.

Piccolo Smallest woodwind instrument having the highest range; similar to the flute but sounding one octave higher. It is a smaller version of the flute.

Pipe organ A large instrument comprised of several keyboards (manuals) and tuned pipes of various sizes. When a key is depressed, air is forced through the pipes and generates pitches.

Pitch Highness or lowness of a musical sound.

Pizzicato Where a performer plucks the strings of violin, viola, cello, or double bass rather than bowing.

Polychoral Vocal or instrumental music for two or more choirs that perform alternately; characteristic of the music performed in St. Mark's Cathedral, Venice, Italy.

Polylingual Multilingual; using several languages in the same composition.

Polyphony (See Counterpoint) A musical texture consisting of two or more melodies played simultaneously.

Polyrhythm More than one rhythm used simultaneously.

Polytextual The simultaneous use of more than one text in a single vocal composition.

Polytonality Two or more keys used simultaneously.

Prelude An introductory piece for a keyboard, usually very short.

Prepared piano A piano in which various objects, such as screws, nuts, bolts, rubber wedges, plastic spoons, are inserted between the strings of a piano; technique attributed to John Cage.

Primitivism A style of music that evolved in the early 20th century that was influenced by primitive works of art from pagan cultures.

Printing Press The printing press, invented by Johann Gutenberg during the Renaissance, changed forever the lives of people in Europe and, eventually, all over the world. Previously, producing books involved copying all the words and illustrations by hand. The labor that went into creating them made each book very expensive. Because Gutenberg's press could produce books quickly and with relatively little effort, producing books became much less expensive, allowing more people to buy reading material.

Program music Instrumental music that tells a story or relates an event; music that is intended to evoke images usually listed in a printed program.

Protestant Reformation A religious movement begun by Martin Luther in the 16th century that was an attempt to reform the Roman Catholic Church; resulted in the founding of Protestant churches. The Protestant Reformation brought new types of religious music including the chorale and psalter.

Psalm An expression of praise to God in the form of poems and prayers; one of the 150 psalms found in the Book of Psalms in the Old Testament of the Bible.

Psalter A collection of psalms set to meter and rhyme.

Ragtime A piano style in which the right hand plays a syncopated melody while the left hand maintains a march-like bass; associated with Scott Joplin.

Recapitulation (See Sonata-allegro form) In sonata-allegro form, the third section which restates the themes introduced in the Exposition.

Recitative (Italian) A type of vocal singing that approximates natural speech inflections accompanied by a keyboard; used in opera, oratorio, and cantata. The words are sung quickly, often on repeated notes, and are used to advance the action of the opera.

Renaissance (French, "rebirth") A period of art and music history ranging from c. 1450 to 1600 and affected by Humanism, which brought a new focus on the importance of human beings and their accomplishments.

Rhythm Movement of music in time with recurring beats and accents.

Rococo (French) An elegant style of art prevalent in France during the mid-18th century. It originated in Paris but was soon adopted throughout France and later in other countries, primarily in Germany and Austria. It is characterized by elegance, and an excessive use of curves in ornamentation. The word Rococo is derived from the French word *rocaille*, which denoted a shell-covered rock.

Romantic Term to describe music of the 19th century. Composers enjoyed looser and more extended forms; a musical composition was viewed as an extension of one's personality.

Rondo form A B A C A B A. A musical form in which the first section recurs between alternating sections; often associated with a multi-movement work.

Round (See Fugue) A melody that may be performed by two or more voices or instruments entering at different times, e.g., "Row, Row, Row Your Boat."

Rubato (Italian, "robbed") A piano technique common during the Romantic period in which the right hand holds back ("robs") and then hurries along ("pays back") the tempo, while the left hand maintains a strict tempo. Done for expressive purposes, this technique typified the piano performances of Frédéric Chopin.

Sacred Connected with God or dedicated to a religious purpose.

Saxophone A single-reed instrument in the woodwind family usually used in jazz bands; not common in orchestras.

Scale An ascending/descending pattern of half steps or whole steps, or both.

Score The notated parts for the instruments of an orchestra or voices in a musical composition.

Secular Relating to worldly things or to things that are not regarded as religious or spiritual.

Sequence A melodic phrase repeated at different pitch levels.

Serialism, serial music Technique of musical composition in the early-mid 20th century which treats the elements of pitch, rhythm, and dynamics in an organized manner; each element recurs in a continually repeated series.

Singspiel (German) Genre of German light opera that consists of songs, spoken dialogue, choruses and instrumental music.

Snare drum A percussion instrument of indefinite pitch. It is in the shape of a small cylinder with skin stretched over each end; a piece of metal mesh is attached to the lower skin which causes a rattling sound when struck.

Sonata (Italian, "sounded") A multi-movement piece to be played on one or more instruments.

Sonata-allegro form The form generally used as the first movement in symphonies and sonatas during the Classic period and early Romantic period. It consisted of Exposition, Development, Recapitulation and Coda. It eventually became known as sonata form.

Song cycle A group of art songs by one composer performed in succession that relates or suggests a story; the texts are often by the same poet.

Song plugger A vocalist or piano player employed by music stores and song publishers in the early 20th century to promote and help sell new sheet music before LP recordings were readily available.

Soprano A high female singing voice.

Sprechstimme, Sprechgesang (German "speech voice, speech song") A vocal style generally associated with the Expressionism movement in which the performer approximates the written pitches on the staff while allowing the voice to "fall away" from the pitch; developed by Arnold Schönberg.

Staff Five horizontal lines and four spaces on which music symbols are placed.

Stanza A group of lines forming the basic recurring metrical unit in a poem; a verse.

String quartet An instrumental ensemble of chamber music which consists of Violin I, Violin II, Viola, and Cello; also, a genre of music consisting of three or four movements arranged for this ensemble.

String family A family of instruments whose sound is produced by vibration of the strings either by plucking or bowing.

Strophic A song form that has two or more stanzas to the same music.

Suite A set of instrumental movements to be performed as a single work; originally arranged from stylized dances for keyboard during the Baroque.

Swing A jazz style that emerged in the 1930s and '40s played mainly by "big bands," characterized by a danceable, bouncy, swing style.

Symphonic poem (See Tone poem) A one-movement work of program music for orchestra in which the music suggests a story, scene, or mood.

Syncopation Placing of accents on weak beats or between beats.

Symphony A large work for orchestra, usually consisting of four movements.

Symphony orchestra A large instrumental ensemble consisting of the four families of instruments: strings, woodwinds, brass, and percussion; the string section is dominant.

Tambourine A percussion instrument of indefinite pitch consisting of a round frame with pairs of small metal plates that jingle; played by shaking or striking.

Tempered Another name for tuned.

Temperament (See Equal temperament)

Tempo The rate of speed at which a musical piece is performed, or relative pace of the music.

Tenor A high male voice.

Terraced dynamics A term used in the Baroque period to describe abrupt changes in dynamic levels; first associated with antiphonal music composed for St. Mark's Cathedral.

Texture (See Homophony, Polyphony) The combination of melodic lines in music.

Text painting, word painting A technique that uses music to describe images in the text, such as a minor key to portray sadness or an ascending scale when the text speaks of rising or climbing.

Theme and Variations Form in which a musical idea or theme recurs but is varied each time in rhythm, harmony or some other feature of the music; usually, the 2nd movement of symphony or sonata.

Through-composed A song that has new music for each stanza.

Timbre The characteristic quality of an instrument or human voice.

Time signature (See Meter)

Timpani A percussion instrument of definite pitch shaped like large copper upside-down kettles; played by mallets. A pedal mechanism changes the pitch; sometimes called kettle drums.

Toccata (Italian) A piece for keyboard or plucked string instrument which features rapid scale passages; gives the impression of an impromptu presentation.

Tonality A system of harmony, based on the major and minor scales of Western music.

Tone A musical sound with a definite pitch.

Tone cluster A chord built on intervals of a 2nd, usually played by the forearm or fist; closely associated with Henry Cowell and Charles Ives.

Tone poem (See Symphonic poem) A one-movement work of program music for orchestra in which the music suggests a story, scene, or mood.

Tonic The first and most important note of a major or minor scale.

Tremolo (Italian) String-playing technique of repeating the same pitch with quick up and down strokes on a violin, viola, cello, or double bass.

Triad A chord which consists of at three tones of intervals of a 3rd ,i.e., C E G of a major scale.

Triangle A percussion instrument of indefinite pitch which consists of a piece of metal bent in the shape of a triangle and suspended from a cord; struck with a metal beater.

Trombone A brass instrument of a moderately low range with a movable slide to change pitch.

Trousers role (See Pants role) A male role, usually for an adolescent, to be performed by a female singer.

Trumpet The highest pitched brass instrument which changes pitch by depressing valves.

Tuba The largest brass instrument with the lowest range that changes pitch by depressing Valves.

Twelve-tone technique A system of atonal music with the 12 chromatic pitches of the scale arranged into a "row" (a pattern) that forms the basis for a music composition.

Verismo (Italian) A style that depicts real life and real situations in 19th-century opera; closely associated with opera composers such as Giacomo Puccini and Giuseppe Verdi.

Vernacular The language that is most widely spoken by ordinary people in a region or country.

Viol A popular bowed, fretted string instrument used during the Renaissance.

Viola A string instrument with a slightly lower range than the violin.

Violin A string instrument with the highest range of the bowed string family.

Virtuoso (Italian) A person who possesses outstanding technical ability in singing or playing an instrument.

Woodwind Family Instrument family made of wood or metal whose sound is produced by vibrations of air in a tube; holes in the tube are opened and closed either by pads or fingers. Some woodwinds are played by blowing across a hole while others are played by blowing air into a mouthpiece which causes a reed or reeds to vibrate. Originally, these instruments were made only of wood.

Xylophone A percussion instrument of definite pitch consisting of flat blocks of wood laid on a frame; blocks are arranged in the shape of a keyboard and are played with wooden mallets.

Study Guide

The date 1450-1600 best describes the approximate dates of the Renaissance. The Renaissance period is known as the Golden Age of Polyphony and can be described by the following characteristics: a cappella, polyphonic, sacred, choral music. The most widely used instrument during the 16th century was a plucked string instrument called the lute.

Martin Luther believed that church music should include songs in the vernacular language as well as in Latin, so he introduced a new kind of hymn called a chorale. As a result of the Protestant Reformation, the Catholic group that advocated reforms within the Catholic Church was the Council of Trent. Their series of meetings over a period of 20 years launched the Counter Reformation.

Musicians date the Baroque period from about 1600 to 1750. The Baroque period was largely a reaction to the Renaissance period and demonstrated a fondness for drama. The Florentine Camerata, centered in Florence, Italy, was a group of intellectuals who promoted changes in musical style that could reflect drama. This new musical style was called monody (solo song) which eventually led to the birth of opera. The first public opera house opened in Venice in 1637.

Claudio Monteverdi was a composer during the early Baroque period who composed in two distinct styles: the polyphonic style of the Renaissance and opera, which reflected the new approach to dramatic music during the Baroque. Monteverdi produced one of the first operas entitled *L'Orfeo*. This new approach to dramatic music included two new vocal forms: recitative and aria. The recitative is a speech-like setting of a text. It is done in declamatory style - very un-melodic - stating the text once.

The aria, which always follows the recitative, is song-like with a melody and a steady rhythm; a portion of the text (as stated in the recitative) is repeated over and over. The recitative and aria are contrasting yet consecutive vocal forms used in passions, oratorios, operas, and cantatas. The proper order of performance is "recitative-aria."

During the Baroque period, the Church of St. Mark in Venice, Italy, designed in the plan of a cross, became the center for the performance of polychoral music. A distinctive feature of Baroque music was the abrupt changes in volume levels called terraced dynamics.

Another major development during the Baroque period was oratorio. The oratorio, based on a religious subject and utilizing the same conventions as opera but without acting and costumes, was originally performed in a prayer chapel during Lent. G.F. Handel's *Messiah* is considered by many to be the world's best-known and best-loved oratorio. This oratorio is reportedly to have been composed in 24 days. King George II rose to his feet during the performance of Handel's "Hallelujah Chorus" from *Messiah*.

J.S. Bach, a primary composer of the Baroque period, wrote five large choral works - only two exist, called passions, i.e., oratorios based upon the events leading to the crucifixion of Christ. He also wrote approximately 200 sacred cantatas, which are basically short oratorios. The term cantata originally meant a piece to be sung. One of J.S. Bach's greatest legacies is a set of 48 preludes and fugues in each of the major and minor keys called *The Well-Tempered Clavier* (The Well-Tuned Keyboard). This piece was composed to demonstrate the effectiveness of a new tuning system. The word clavier is a generic term for any keyboard instrument. Bach was a very religious and dedicated composer who habitually wrote *SDG* (*Soli Deo Gloria*, "To God Alone be Glory"), *JJ (Jesu, Juva)*, "Jesus, Help"), and *INJ (In Nomine Jesu,* "In the Name of Jesus") on his compositions. His music is catalogued according to BWV (Bachwerkverzeichniss).

Polyphony prevailed during the Baroque period. The fugue is an imitative polyphonic composition with three to five melodic lines or "voices." A round is an example of polyphonic texture. A major device in composition during the Baroque period was the concept of text painting or word painting. This technique is the use of certain devices in music to describe or express the text.

In the Baroque period, musicians began composing large works consisting of several movements. The concerto grosso, usually consisting of three movements, was a major development during the Baroque period. A concerto grosso is described as a string orchestra along with a small group of solo instruments. *The Four Seasons* is a concerto grosso and was composed by Antonio Vivaldi. Later, the concerto grosso evolved into the solo concerto, simply referred to as concerto. This involved a symphony orchestra with solo instruments such as violin, flute, viola or some other solo instrument.

The Rococo was a sub-period that overlapped the latter part of the Baroque and the first part of the Classic period. It was centered largely in France initially. The music of the Rococo was generally light and entertaining rather than serious and dramatic. Music performed by a relatively small number of people in a small room is called chamber music. Chamber music is best described as music for a small instrumental ensemble that is generally performed in a small setting with one instrument to a part.

The Classic period (1750-1825) can be described by the following terms: clarity, reason, restraint, and form. During the Classic period, artists found beauty in form and symmetry of design; composers began to use more expressive dynamics, i.e., crescendos and decrescendos; and instrumental music clearly dominated the period. Among instrumental genres, the symphony experienced the greatest development and offered composers the widest field for creativity.

The symphony is a multi-movement orchestral work, consisting generally of four movements. Some of the most common instrumental forms used in symphonies in the Classic period were: 1st movement - sonata-allegro; 2nd movement - theme and variations; 3rd movement - minuet and trio; and 4th movement - rondo or sonata-allegro.

The Classic sonata-allegro form, usually the first movement of a symphony, was generally conceived as a three-part structure - ABA. The individual sections of the sonata-allegro form are named the Exposition, Development, Recapitulation and Coda.

In the Classic period, the use of polyphonic texture decreased; homophonic texture dominated. A hymn sung with accompaniment is an example of homophonic texture. A Classic multi-movement composition to be "sounded" by one or two instruments is called a sonata.

Two outstanding composers of the Classic period were Franz Josef Haydn and Wolfgang Amadeus Mozart. Haydn, considered by his peers to be the "father of the symphony," enjoyed a successful relationship with a patron, the Esterházy family for nearly 28 years. He composed over 104 symphonies; two of his most famous symphonies are nicknamed "Surprise" and "Farewell." His most famous oratorio is entitled *The Creation*, which is believed by many to be second only to *Messiah,* by G.F. Handel. His works are catalogued according to Hob. numbers (Hoboken), named after Anthony Hoboken who catalogued them. Mozart, one of history's most tragic figures, died as a pauper at age 35. A child genius, he began composing his first symphonies around age 13. He is probably best known for his opera *The Marriage of Figaro.* He composed approximately 50 symphonies. His works are catalogued according to K. numbers, named after Ludwig von Köchel, who catalogued his works.

The Romantic period (1825-1900) was marked by a time of expansion, mystery, and emotion. Feelings began to replace reason. Composers were concerned about what later generations would think of them. One's art was considered an extension of themselves. Society was intrigued by unknown, faraway, exotic places. Some of their favorite subjects were the forest, witches, warlocks, the spirit world, and mythology.

Ludwig van Beethoven, who had the reputation of being the best pianist in Vienna, was afflicted in his late twenties with an ear disease that eventually led to total deafness. His *Symphony No. 5* has a theme that consists of only four notes. His *Symphony No. 9* is sometimes referred to as the "Choral Symphony," since it calls for a choir in the last movement.

Beethoven is considered one of the few transitional composers, living and working in both the Classic and Romantic periods. He was the first composer to successfully earn his living apart from the Patronage System.

Piotr Ilyich Tchaikovsky, Russian composer, is well remembered for his ballets *The Nutcracker, Swan Lake,* and *The Sleeping Beauty.* One of his most memorable compositions is *The 1812 Overture* which was commissioned to be performed at the inauguration of "Christ Our Redeemer Church" which was built to celebrate Russia's victory over Napoleon in 1812.

Felix Mendelssohn, Romantic composer, was one of the most prolific composers of this time. He and his sister, Fanny, grew up in a home well-endowed with exposure to the arts. He is probably best known for *A Mid-Summer Night's Dream*, composed when he was 17 years of age. He also composed the oratorios *St. Paul* and *Elijah.* Mendelssohn is credited for reviving interest in the music of J.S. Bach by performing Bach's *St. Matthew Passion.*

Giuseppe Verdi, considered by many to be the "greatest of the Romantic operatic masters," was eventually elected to the Italian Parliament.His name "VERDI" was shouted throughout the streets by the public who were acclaiming "Vittorio Emmanuel Re d' Italia," the future king of Italy. One of his most famous operas is *Aïda*, which was reportedly written to celebrate the inauguration of the Suez Canal in 1871. Other popular operas by Verdi are *Rigoletto* and *La Traviata.*

Giacomo Puccini, another of the great masters of Italian Romantic opera, was a proponent of verismo, reflecting realism or naturalism in opera. One of his greatest operas is entitled *La Boheme.* Another popular opera by Puccini during this time period is *Turandot.* In this opera a Chinese princess invites young men to guess the answers to three riddles. If they guess correctly, she agrees to marry them; if not, they are executed. A famous aria from *Turandot* is "Nessun dorma."

Richard Wagner is the composer of a series of Romantic period operas entitled *Der Ring des Nibelungen.* In this cycle of operas, Wagner incorporated gesamtkunstwerk, (union of all the arts). He designed and constructed the Bayreuth Theater for the performance of his operas which he called "music dramas." He placed the orchestra in a pit over which the audience had an unobstructed view of the stage, which has become the custom in opera houses ever since. In music, the term leitmotif means using melodic fragments to represent emotions, objects, or persons in his operas.

Comic opera in Italy was known as opera buffa; in Germany, Singspiel; in France, opera comique, in England, ballad opera.

Franz Schubert is known primarily for his art songs, having composed approximately 600. One of his best-known compositions is the art song the *Erlking.* In the *Erlking,* the singer portrays four characters: the Narrator, the Father, the Child, and the Erlking. The art song is the complete melding of the music, text, and piano so that none is more important than the other. The term universally applied to art songs is lieder (lied, singular).

The Romantic period composer Robert Schumann had a promising career as a concert pianist until he injured two fingers of his right hand with an exercise apparatus. He also suffered from "multiple personalities," some of which were named Florestan, Eusebius, and Mr. Raro. He is known primarily for art songs including several song cycles, one of which is *Dichterliebe*, which he dedicated to his bride, Clara, in 1840.

Franz Liszt is widely recognized as one of the first "personality performers" and was the first pianist to change the position of the piano so the audience could see his face. He is considered one of the great virtuoso pianist-composers of the Romantic period. He is noted for his difficult, almost un-playable, passages in his piano works. In addition to his compositions for piano, he contributed to the genre program music with his tone poems (symphonic poems).

Frédéric Chopin, Romantic period composer, wrote almost exclusively for the piano. His playing style helped develop the technique known as rubato (Italian "robbed), in which the right hand "robs" the beat by pushing forward or holding back while the left hand maintains a strict tempo.

During the 1860s, a movement began in France known as Symbolism in literature and Impressionism in painting and music. This movement was somewhat a reaction to the Romantic period and sought to "give an impression or suggestion" of an idea, object or experience. Details were elusive, vague. Claude Debussy represents the epitome of composers of Impressionism. His music evokes a dreamy, hazy atmosphere. Even though he never abandoned tonality (key), he nonetheless obscured it, sometimes alternating between major and minor keys. The name "Impressionism" took hold based upon Claude Monet's 1872 painting, *Impression, Sunrise*.

Primitivism proved to be a significant movement during the early 1900s by producing one of the masterpieces of modern music. This movement grew out of fascination for the cultures of Africa as Europeans began invading and conquering portions of Africa. Added to this was the United States pressing westward into the Western Plains thereby becoming exposed to the culture of the Native American. Igor Stravinsky best represents this time period with his ballet *The Rite of Spring*, which caused a riot at its premier in Paris in 1913. *The Rite of Spring* is based upon a brutal human sacrifice of a young maiden to appease the fertility gods.

A late 19th-century and early 20th -century musical style that resulted from explorations of the subconscious mind was called Expressionism. This concept was inspired by the musings of Sigmund Freud and portrayed society as distorted and disturbed. The painting *The Scream* by Edvard Munch is widely identified with this movement. Arnold Schönberg's *Pierrot Lunaire* is a collection of 21 poems and depicts the uneasiness of this time period. He made use of a vocal device called Sprechstimme or Sprechgesang - a melodramatic type of singing halfway between speaking and singing in which the pitch is not sustained but is allowed to either rise or fall.

Early in the 20th century composers began to feel that "all musical combinations, all harmonies, all rhythms have been composed - there is nothing left." This led to a new development referred to as Experimentalism. Essential to this period is Charles Ives. His music is filled with multiple, simultaneous keys and rhythms, tone clusters (occasionally played by a 14 ½ inch board), and "off-key" sounds (bands playing simultaneously in two different keys).

John Cage is perhaps the most daring experimenter who favored aleatory music (music of chance). He is best known for 4'33" and for a series of pieces called *Imaginary Landscapes* (12 radios on stage). Cage also devised a means of expanding the possibilities of the piano by utilizing wood, screws, nuts, bolts, rubber wedges placed strategically between the piano strings. This technique is referred to as "prepared piano." Also, in this period of Experimentalism, Pauline Oliveros composed music for the voice in a non-traditional style using abstract sounds such as sh, z, p, t along with tongue clicks. This piece is called *Sound Patterns*.

Also in the 20th century, composers began to express a certain kind of nationalism that reflected the music of African Americans. William Grant Still figures prominently in this group. He was the first African American to have a symphony performed by a major orchestra and the first to have an opera produced by a major American opera company, as well as an opera broadcast on nation-wide television. His symphony entitled *Afro-American Symphony* makes use of a banjo, which is considered a non-orchestral instrument.

Regarding opera in the 20th century, the best-known of all American operas is *Porgy and Bess*, composed by George Gershwin. One of the most popular 20th -century musicals is *West Side Story* by Leonard Bernstein. Set in New York, it retells the story of Romeo and Juliet and deals with tension between two rival street gang wars.

Jazz, which originated in America, is considered purely American with few non-American influences. Its roots lie deep within the African American culture.

Ragtime is considered a "pre-jazz" style and is also deeply rooted within the African American culture. Within this style, syncopation - playing against the beat or playing off beat - plays an important role. *Maple Leaf Rag,* by Scott Joplin, is perhaps one of the best-known ragtime pieces of all time. It was named for a night club located in Sedalia, Missouri, where Joplin performed. He became known as "the king of rag."

Blues is an American type of folk music that evolved in the American south during the mid-1800s. Considered a form of jazz, blues gained popularity in the early 1900s through recordings of well-known blues singers such as Mamie Smith, Bessie Smith, Rosetta Tharp, and B. B. King.

Many people during this time preferred a quieter kind of music which became known as "swing band" music. This style appealed to white, middle-class Americans and rapidly swept across America around the end of the Great Depression. Typical of this style were musicians such as Benny Goodman, Tommy Dorsey, and Glenn Miller.

Country music can be traced back to Appalachian folk music around the turn of the 20th century with Jimmie Rodgers and the Carter Family. Bill Monroe, the "Father of Bluegrass" first popularized bluegrass which was named after his band, "Bill Monroe and the Blue Grass Boys." Later artists include Hank Williams, Chet Atkins, Jim Reeves, Patsy Cline, Willie Nelson, Merle Haggard, and Johnny Cash.

Rock and Roll evolved during the 1950s from a union of two styles of singing: rhythm and blues and country music. In 1955, Bill Haley and the Comets recorded "Rock Around the Clock. This new style of singing was made popular by singers like Buddy Holly, Elvis Presley, Little Richard, Jerry Lee Lewis, Fats Domino, and Chuck Berry.

In 1964, The Beatles, made their US debut in America. The reception of the Beatles by American audiences opened the door for other British groups, such as The Rolling Stones, to come to America.

Bibliography

Burkholder, J. Peter, Grout, Donald J., and Palisca, Claude V. *Concise History of Western Music*, 4th ed. New York, NY: W. W. Norton & Company, 1998.

Britannica, The Editors of Encyclopedia. "Country music". Encyclopedia Britannica, 10 Dec. 2022, https://www.britannica.com/art/country-music. Accessed 9 February 2023.

Kot, Greg. "Rock and roll". ENCYCLOPEDIA BRITANNICA, 9 Dec. 2022, https://www.britannica.com/art/rock-and-roll-early-style-of-rock-music. Accessed 4 March 2023.

Lebrecht, Norman. *The Book of Musical Anecdotes*. New York, NY: The Free Press, 1985.

Manheim, Steven. *Blues Musicians of the Mississippi Delta*. Charleston, SC: Arcadia Publishing, 2019.

Menard, Louis. *The Elvic Oracle*. https://www.newyorker.com/magazine/2015/11/16/the-elvic-oracle.

Randel, Don Michael. *The Harvard Biographical Dictionary of Music*. Cambridge, MA: The Belknap Press of Harvard University Press, 1996.

Randel, Don Michael. *The New Harvard Dictionary of Music*, 8th ed. Cambridge, MA: The Belknap Press of Harvard University Press, 1986.

Sadie, Stanley, ed. The *New Grove Dictionary of Music and Musicians*. London: Oxford University Press, 2004.

Scholes, Percy A. The *Oxford Companion to Music,* 8th ed. London: Oxford University Press, 1950.

Stolle, Roger. *Hidden History of Mississippi Blues*. Charleston, SC: The History Press, 2011.

Thompson, Oscar, ed. The *International Cyclopedia of Music and Musicians,* 9th ed. New York, NY: Dodd, Mead & Company, 1964.

World's Greatest Music, Classic *fm. Beethoven: Compositions, Biography, Siblings and More Facts.* Accessed 4 March 2023.

Wright, Craig. *Music in Western Civilization.* Boston, MA: Schirmer Cengage Learning, 2010.

Made in the USA
Las Vegas, NV
11 December 2023

82562571R00075